The

MINIMALIST WOODWORKER

ESSENTIAL TOOLS & SMART SHOP IDEAS
for BUILDING WITH LESS

Publisher: Paul McGahren
Editor: Matthew Teague
Design: Lindsay Hess
Layout: Michael Douglas
Photography: Vic Tesolin
Illustration: Carolyn Mosher
Copyeditor: Kerri Grzybicki

Spring House Press
3613 Brush Hill Court
Nashville, TN 37216

ISBN: 978-1940611358
Library of Congress Control Number: 2015954653
Printed in the United States of America
Second Printing: May 2016

Note: The following list contains names used in *The Minimalist Woodworker*
that may be registered with the United States Copyright Office:
Workmate; Disston D-28; Robertson; Clapham's Beeswax Polish

The information in this book is presented in good faith; however, no warranty is
given, nor are results guaranteed. Woodworking is inherently dangerous. Your
safety is your responsibility. Neither Spring House Press nor the author assume any
responsibility for any injuries or accidents.

To learn more about Spring House Press books, or to find
a retailer near you, email info@springhousepress.com
or visit us at: www.springhousepress.com.

The

MINIMALIST
WOODWORKER

ESSENTIAL TOOLS & SMART SHOP IDEAS
for BUILDING WITH LESS

VIC TESOLIN

SPRING HOUSE PRESS

For my girls, Christina and Alex.
Thanks for keeping me sane . . . a big job, I know.

Knowledge is only a rumor until it is in the muscle.
— PAPUA NEW GUINEA PROVERB

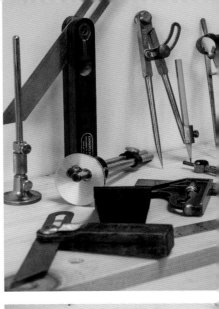

CONTENTS

FOREWORD
BY TOM FIDGEN

the minimalist woodworker . . .
Ok.
Woodworker.
Most of us can relate to that part, but minimalist?
Let's break it down to the bare essentials;
bring it back to the core.
Here's what the dictionary says:

minimal
adjective
Of a minimum amount, quantity, or degree
In art it's characterized by the use of simple forms or structures
In music, it's characterized by the repetition and gradual
alteration of short phrases

Here's my interpretation . . .

minimal
That's where we all begin—
naked and screaming.
I think it's a good place to start, don't you?
Can you stay that way when you grow up?
Probably not the best idea.
Can you live and work with a minimal mind set and practice?
Of course you can—
but it may be a little more difficult than you think.
Thankfully, Vic just made the workshop waters a little easier to navigate.

You'd think it would be easy, this whole minimal thing,
getting rid of the waste and the distractions.
But the hard truth is this:
we've gotten used to having more.
Having plenty . . .
having too much!
Not always physically, on the shelf and on the floor,
but in the dust bin between your ears—
that's where it begins.

We all have the ability to walk the path less travelled.
We can choose to say no, whenever we're ready.
We can make, instead of buy.
We can fix it, instead of re-purchasing.
Again and again, over and over.

So to the minimalist thinker, the minimalist worker,
the minimalist woodworker—

Break it all down to the basics—
breath in, breath out, one foot in front of the other.
Choose your battles.
Think long and hard before you bring something into your home
and into your life—
and don't forget the workspace!

From the wood you use in your woodshop;
where you get it, how it's harvested.
The tools you hold in your hands.
Even the joinery you use to hold your work together . . .
how long do you think it will last?
Does it matter?
It certainly should, for you—as the maker.
Will someone need to replace those things?
Those tools?
That bench?
Is it an improvement?
Can we do a little better?
This book will help.

minimal.

If not literally in the toolkit, then metaphorically in the spirit of the craft.
The minimalist woodworker—
I raise my glass!

"Make everyday a masterpiece."

—Tom Fidgen,
The Unplugged Woodshop-Toronto, October 2015

INTRODUCTION

The truth about woodworking is that you don't need a single machine or power tool to woodwork. There, I said it. What you do need is about 40 square feet of space for a workbench and some hand tools. That's all you need to start making projects out of wood. You can work with even less space if you just want to make boxes, spoons, or other small projects but 40 square feet is a good start.

And that's a good thing. Some of us have little room to work with. Living in apartments, condominiums, and town homes means that we don't necessarily have the space for a conventional wood shop. Even roomy homes have basements and garages that share space with cars and family overflow. The typical machines found in stand-alone shops are not possible to use in these smaller spaces. And can you imagine the backlash you would get from a neighbor in an apartment building if you fired up a router and a shop vacuum?

WOODWORKING VS. WOOD MACHINING

Machines have become a mainstream staple available to almost any consumer at many different price points. They are so ubiquitous that you can find them at home centers. And the common belief is that they are required to woodwork.

I must admit that machines are handy, but they aren't necessary. Machines, to my mind, are modern-day apprentices. They do the tasks that I don't want to do. For example, a thickness planer speeds up the process of dimensioning lumber . . . but I don't need one to get the job done. Machines are also quite adept at repeating operations, which makes them well-suited to production work. If you have to make 25 tables it makes sense to spend the time to set up a machine to cut the joinery. But what if you are only making one table? In many cases it doesn't make sense at all. Most of us are not production woodworkers so why have the production tools?

I think we were lulled into the myth that power tools are more accurate than hand tools. In some cases this may be true but machines still need to be tuned and maintained to retain their accuracy. My question is—how accurate do you need to be? One of the characteristics of wood is that it is always taking on and losing water via the humidity in the air. A freshly dimensioned board can change over the time it takes to eat lunch so why pull out the calipers and micrometers to check dimensions? I think people feel that they can compensate for a lack of experience by trying to work to ultra-high tolerances to ensure success. I once had a student who was concerned when making a tabletop that one corner was thicker by 0.004"! That is the thickness of a piece of printer paper.

The machines I choose to keep in my shop save me hours of hard labor but in the end, I could drop them all and still be able to woodwork.

THE POWER OF THE HOBBYIST

I hear many woodworkers describe themselves as 'only a hobbyist' when asked about what they do in the shop. The part I take exception with is the 'only.' Hobbyists think for some reason that they aren't as qualified as a woodworker if they are not making money at it. I happen to think that some of the best woodworkers are those who don't have the pressures of running a business looming constantly over their heads like a dark cloud. When I made furniture for a living I was constantly stressed about finishing one job and lining up the next one in order to make ends meet. Being a hobbyist allows you the freedom to explore new things and try new techniques without worrying about putting food on the table. You can spend time actually mastering skills. And if something doesn't work out you can drill a hole in it and call it a birdhouse.

About three years ago I started experimenting with axes—not juggling them while they're on fire but using them as a way to remove material quickly. It took some time to learn how to sharpen and use axes but after some blood (literally) and sweat I worked it out. Now I use axes quite often in my shop. The point is, I would not have had the time to try this new (to me) technique if I were woodworking for a living. I would have stuck with my same old techniques because you don't get paid to experiment.

HAND TOOLS—A LOVE AFFAIR?

The majority of the tools in my shop do not have a motor on them. I do this because I enjoy using them. I'm not intrigued by the romance of them. I don't care who made them or when. I pick tools that get the job done.

Hand tools produce little dust and noise, which makes them perfectly suited for small, in-home spaces or for people who don't want the constant din of motors running. After spending 14 years in the Canadian Artillery, the last thing I want is more noise.

Many worry about the learning curve associated with hand tools. But believe me: If you can set up a router to cut a mortise you can use hand tools. What you do need to do, however, is practice using them. But once you produce your first gossamer-thin shaving with a well-tuned hand plane, you'll find the time to make more. And then you'll no longer have to sand machine marks out of your projects. I wonder if anyone thinks fondly about the next time they have to sand something? I doubt it. Your family will miss you but they will know where to find you.

PROJECTS FOR THE SHOP

The projects in this book were selected to help you get into using hand tools. There are jigs and fixtures, shop furniture, and storage projects that will help you get started. Each project has its own set of skills that will add to your repertoire and each skill is transferable to almost any other project you can dream up. The mortise and tenon joint you cut for the saw bench and bent is the same joints you will use time and time again to make furniture.

The other advantage to starting with shop projects is if they don't turn out with perfect-looking joinery, no one will see it but you. A small gap in a joint reveal or a bit of planing tear-out can be tolerated in a shop project. The key is to learn from those oopsies and do a better job next time.

Please note that this is not the only way to woodwork. This is the way I woodwork. But I feel that my techniques will get you good results. The techniques and projects in this book come right out of my own shop. These techniques are not new; in fact, many of them are thousands of years old, though we all but abandoned them a century ago when machines became all the rage.

Over years of practice I separated the wheat from chaff and have come up with a way to woodwork that makes it easy and enjoyable. So let's stop talking about woodworking and head into the shop to make something.

In order to understand, you must do.

Chapter 1

A SPACE TO WORK

When you think 'wood shop,' you normally think of a fairly big space with lots of tools on the walls, machines on the floor, and wood everywhere. This is just one type of shop but it's the one we see all the time in books and magazines. My shop used to look like that until I started to go the Minimalist route.

There are plenty of us out there who don't install the table saw first and then try to cram everything else in around it, especially when space is a premium. What if I suggested starting with enough space for a 20" x 60" workbench and some hand tools? Would you have enough room then? My first shop space was 40 square feet located under the basement stairs. I wasn't able to stand erect in the first third of the shop but I had a pegboard wall and tool storage under the bench. I wasn't making large things but I was making something. Now when I look at my 170 square foot shop, in comparison, I feel like I have tons of space.

So what am I trying to say here? You don't need a big space to make things out of wood. The truth is you can woodwork almost anywhere. Whether that is a basement, garage, pantry, or spare room, embrace the space you have and work within it. You may have only a stout kitchen table and an understanding spouse. That will work fine. The point is that a lack of square footage should not stop you from woodworking. There are always two things a woodworker wants: more clamps and more space. However, if all you've got is 100 square feet, use it.

We'll talk about tools in more depth and why I chose what I did in the next chapter. For now, let's take a look at a few different minimalist shop layouts. If your space doesn't match one of these, you can likely draw from these ideas to create your own home workshop.

MY HUMBLE GARAGE IS MORE THAN ENOUGH

I'm fortunate to have 170 square feet of space to house my shop. When I started in this garage space, I had all the power tools and machines I thought I needed. Things are a lot different now, after I've realized that most of those machines are unnecessary to the kind of work I enjoy. The few machines I still have fit easily in the space and do come in handy. But the truth is that the power tools I do have don't see nearly as much work as my hand tools. The layout of my own shop is pretty straightforward, which helps keep work efficient.

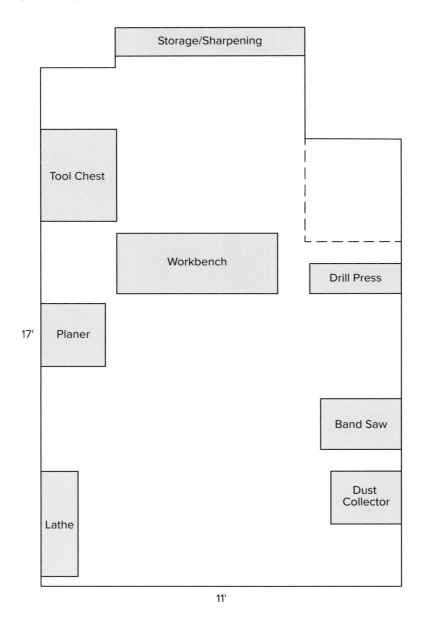

SPACE UNDER THE STAIRS IS ALL YOU NEED

Many multi-floor homes—be they traditional houses, downtown condos, or rented rooms—feature little alcoves under the stairs. Jeff lives in a loft-style downtown apartment. Under the stairs to the top floor is an area that was free so he put a workspace there. Jeff works with hand tools so this space is perfect. Hand planes and saws make fairly coarse shavings so he doesn't have to worry too much about dust getting flung into the other areas of his apartment.

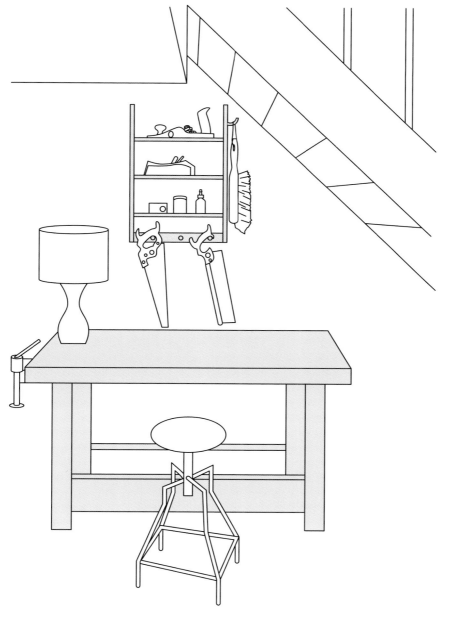

SIMPLY WORK IN THE LIVING ROOM

Whether in a cramped studio or the corner of any living room, adding a place to work requires little space. Evan's small bachelor apartment doesn't have a ton of room in it but when you're resolved to work with your hands, you make room. The small bench is up against the wall and tools get stored in nearby drawers and on the shelf under the bench. Evan is a timber framer and a heritage carpenter by training. But in his urban apartment workspace he makes spoons with hand tools. In this space, a large window by the bench provides the natural light any woodworker craves. The same spare concept would work well in almost any home.

A simple hole in the benchtop is outfitted with a stop that helps secure work in place.

A bench stop and simple body weight stabilize a panel when handplaning an edge.

Spoons and other utensils are frequent projects in Evan's apartment workspace, but boxes or other small projects are possible as well.

UTILIZE YOUR UTILITY ROOM

When all you have in a finished basement is the utility room, then that's where you go. Ken has managed to make a functional shop in about 100 square feet that includes even a table saw. You have to be fastidious about organization in a space this small. The old adage 'a place for everything and everything in its place' takes on a whole new meaning here. Ken turns out smaller projects like occasional tables, bookcases, and boxes with ease. In a similar setup, simple hanging shelves or pegboards are an easy solution.

In tight quarters it's even more important to have a place for everything. A tool cabinet and chest house Ken's hand tools neatly in one corner.

With enough planning, a small space transforms into a well-equipped shop that even includes basic power tools.

Regardless of the type of woodworking you enjoy, a stable work bench is at the heart of any shop.

GOOD LIGHTING IS A MUST

If you decide to go hand tools only, then the only electrical you will need is lighting. The most efficient type of lighting is fluorescent tubes but II prefer LED lighting, which is becoming more affordable everyday. Either way, look for general lighting that will illuminate the space and task lighting to augment the overall lighting. Task lighting fixtures can be had inexpensively so don't be afraid to set them up wherever you need it.

My shop has a few machines so I run 110 volt power on 20 amp breakers to make sure that I don't blow a circuit. This pretty standard electrical setup allows me to run my small dust collector in tandem with a tool.

Flourescent lighting no longer means buzzing fixtures. Even inexpensive fixtures allow warm light designed to replicate natural light.

Smaller power tools like grinders often come with light fixtures built in. If not, inexpensive magnetic fixtures can be easily added.

Mobile and adjustable, directional LED light fixtures offer an easy fix when work requires a closer look.

HEAT AND AIR KEEP IT COMFORTABLE

In warm climates a simple window unit air conditioner may be all you need to tamp down humidity and keep it cool.

Having the ability to control the temperature and humidity in the shop is certainly nice. If you are working in a basement or elsewhere in the house, you will benefit from the conditions in the house, which are usually great for woodworking. My shop is in a fully insulated attached garage. The insulation makes it easy to heat in the winter, which is pretty important up here in Canada where -30°C isn't uncommon. A small 220-volt construction heater takes care of all my heating needs. I can keep the shop at a cool 50°F most of the time so that glue and finish doesn't freeze. I usually only pump up the heat for glue-ups and finish applications. I don't worry too much about being cold because working primarily by hand gets the blood pumping.

Northern climates might require only a small space heater to keep you warm. Adding a little physical work with hand tools never hurts, either.

In the summer it can get up to 30°C outside but the insulated space only gets to around 25°C. I find that the killer in the summer is the humidity so I keep a dehumidifier in the space to keep it around 50 percent humidity. Just reducing the humidity makes it comfortable to work and my tools don't turn orange either.

It's also good to have some way to ventilate the shop so that you aren't breathing in fumes from finishes. I simply open the garage door and put a box fan in the gap to exhaust things. You can also install a ventilation fan like those found in a bathroom to get the job done.

In larger spaces, PTAC units, like those found in many hotel rooms, do a great job of both heating and cooling.

QUICK AND EASY FLOORING SOLUTIONS

The ideal flooring for any workshop is a wooden floor. They are much more comfortable to stand on than most alternatives, but wooden floors simply aren't possible in every situation. My shop has a peel-and-stick type of floor that makes sweeping up a breeze. I'm still working on concrete but after an hour or so of planing, I'm ankle-deep in wood shavings that I stand on. An anti-fatigue mat is a great option behind the bench, where you do a lot of standing.

Wood floors for a shop don't need to be fancy, Simple plywood or underlayment can be purchased in sheet form and set into place.

Rubber flooring mats or tiles add a little bounce and comfort to concrete floors and are much more forgiving on the edges of dropped tools.

Chapter 2

TOOLS IN THE SMALL SHOP

O nce you settle on a space for your shop, it's time to start filling it with tools—just the ones you really need. The most important tool for a minimalist woodworker is a workbench. When working with machines, you take the wood to the machine. Conversely with hand tools, you bring the tool to the wood. So what you need is a solid, flat surface that will hold your work. You also need a few work holding devices to secure the wood on the bench so it can be more easily worked.

Building the bench you see at left is covered in chapter 8. This design is easy to build and works well in any shop. In the absence of a bench, you can get by using a portable workbench like a Workmate. In fact, the first few projects in this book are made on a bench of this type. They're inexpensive and available at any home center. Once you have a few projects under your belt, you'll be ready to tackle the workbench.

Whether you're just starting to woodwork or are approaching the craft with a renewed interest in handwork, it's important to start with the tools you need and become comfortable with how they work. In a small space, only a few tools are truly required.

In this chapter I outline a set of hand tools that would accomodate almost any project you might want to tackle. Some of these tools are key to any shop. Others make nice additions for certain types of work. The key is to start small. Become comfortable with a small set of tools and techniques. You may then want or need others. Or realize, as I do time and time again, that less really is more.

Hand Tools

The backbone of minimalist woodworking is hand tools. Over the next few pages I take you through the essential tools that you should start with. By no means do these tools need to be all brand-new. There are many options for the fledgling woodworker from vintage tools to freshly minted tools from a modern tool maker. I use a combination of old and new tools. When well-tuned, both work just fine. For each of the following sections I lay out what is essential but also include tools that are nice to have. Let's take a look at what goes into a basic minimalist tool kit.

PLANES

Planes are the work horses in the minimalist shop. They are responsible for important tasks like flattening, smoothing, and cutting joinery. The basic planes can be broken up into a couple of different categories: bench planes and joinery planes.

Bench Planes

Bench planes are mainly used for flattening and dimensioning stock, and preparing surfaces for finish.

FLATTENING & SMOOTHING — WHAT'S THE DIFFERENCE?

At first blush flattening and smoothing may appear to be the same thing. The difference really has to do with the quality of the surface. Flattening means that you are getting a surface flat and aren't overly concerned about the quality of the surface itself. Once you have one flat face, you can move on to thicknessing or squaring an edge. However, just because a surface is flat doesn't mean that it is ready for finish. This is where smoothing comes in. Smoothing is what you do to get surfaces ready for finishing. In power tool terms, smoothing is what you would do with a random orbital sander, just without the dust, noise, and a numb hand.

Jack Plane

The most useful size of bench plane is known as the #5 or jack plane. As the name suggests, this Jack-of-all-trades is suited for many tasks. If you're just starting out, this is the plane to start with. A jack plane is long enough to flatten most stock yet not too long to use as a smoother. It is also the perfect size for using on its side with a shooting board to trim the end-grain of boards.

Jack Plane

More Key Bench Planes

You can get an awful lot of work done with a jack but there are three other sizes of bench planes that I use.

Jointer

The jointer (a #7 or #8) is a long plane that will allow you to joint long edges and flatten large surfaces with ease. The longer the plane the flatter the surface it will create.

Smoother

The #4 smoother is a smaller plane than the jack. The plane is a bit lighter and easier to maneuver on the surface that you're preparing for finish. I like using wooden smoothers because the wooden sole of the plane burnishes the surface you are smoothing, making it shine even before finishing.

Block Plane

In addition to these two planes you can also use a small, one-handed block plane. Block planes are specifically designed to work on end-grain. They typically have a low-angle blade bed, which means that the blade is inserted bevel up. Block planes are good for small trimming jobs, softening hard edges, and other small tasks at the bench.

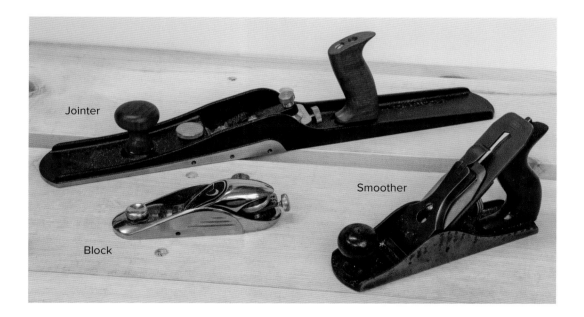

Jointer

Smoother

Block

SETTING UP YOUR BENCH PLANES

Success with hand planes requires a bit of work And like anything else, you must know the steps required to set up the tools. Regardless of the type of planes you own, all are set up and adjusted in a similar manner.

PLANE ADJUSTMENT

The two most common bench plane adjusters are the Stanley-style adjuster and the Norris-type adjuster. In the case of a Stanley-type adjuster, there is a wheel that controls the depth-of-cut and a separate lateral adjustment lever that controls the position of the blade in the mouth of the plane. The Norris-type adjuster has both the depth-of-cut and the lateral adjustment in one adjuster mechanism. Twisting the knob clockwise or counterclockwise adjusts the depth of cut and pushing the same adjuster left or right adjusts the blade laterally.

There are many techniques for setting up a plane for use. The method I use gets quick results and you never run the risk of taking off too much material on the first pass.

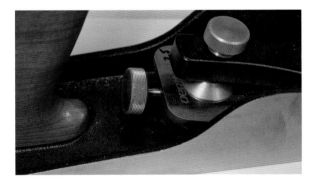

Hand planes are simple tools with only a few moving parts and adjusters. Loosening the knurled knob on top allows you to adjust the blade right or left and secure it in place.

The rear knob on a Stanley-style plane adjusts the blade forward and backward and has a separate lateral adjuster.

AIM FOR UNIFORM SHAVINGS

1 Sight the blade in the mouth of the plane from the bottom and ensure that it looks centered in the opening. If the blade appears to be higher on one side than the other, move the adjuster toward the side that is high.

2 Retract the blade and place the plane on the surface of the wood and start working it back and forth, while slowly turning the depth-of-cut adjuster clockwise. Keep an eye on the mouth to see where the shaving is starting to emerge. If the shaving comes out left or right of center, move the lateral adjuster to the side it's cutting.

3 With the shaving centered in the mouth, adjust the depth of cut until you produce uniform shavings of your desired thickness. Thin shavings might be slower at removing stock but they allow you to create a smooth surface more easily.

Joinery Planes

These planes eliminate the need for things like power routers and table saws. They remove material in a controlled, precise manner. And with the absence of a motor, your shop remains quiet while using them.

Shoulder Plane

Shoulder Plane

This plane excels at trimming the shoulders of a tenon but by no means is that all it can do. Using overlapping passes, you can trim the cheeks of a tenon to sneak up on a perfect fit. Shoulder planes can also be used for cutting rabbets with the grain.

Plow Plane

The plow is designed to create grooves that run with the grain. This is an often-created element of joinery that ranges from letting in a drawer bottom for a drawer to creating tongue-and-groove joinery. A good plow, either old or new, should have a sturdy fence and a depth stop to help control the groove dimensions. A plow can also cut a rabbet with the grain.

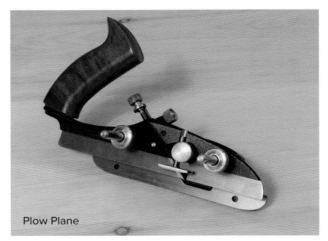
Plow Plane

Router Plane

The router plane earns its keep by precisely removing material to a specified depth. The bottom surfaces of joints like the dado and

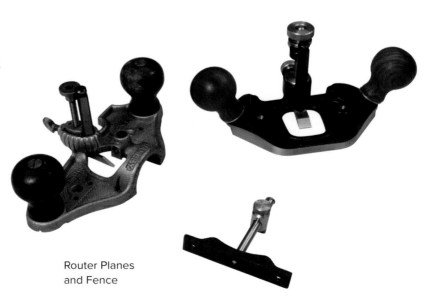
Router Planes
and Fence

Rabbet Plane

SAWS

Saws are essential to the minimalist woodworker. They allow the user to break down lumber to the proper width and length, as well as cutting joinery. There are three main saws that I wouldn't do without.

Panel Saw

My favorite panel saw is a vintage Disston D-28. The saw has 10 ppi (points per inch) and is filed with a rip-type tooth known as a hybrid tooth, which works well for both ripping and cross-cutting. In fact, most rip saws with teeth sized 10 ppi and smaller will work just fine with and across the grain.

the hinge mortise that need to be flat are easy work for the router. This tool also does a fine job at removing the waste for inlays and banding.

Nice to Have: The Rabbet Plane

The rabbet plane is designed to cut rabbets both with and across the grain. Most rabbet planes will have a nicker ahead of the main cutter that pre-scores the shoulder of the rabbet ensuring that the cut is clean and doesn't tear out. A sturdy fence and a depth stop are pretty convenient when it comes to this plane. Another great feature is a skewed blade. This further reduces the chance of blowout when working across the grain and creates a surprisingly smooth surface.

Back Saw

As the name suggests, these saws have a back on them to help keep them stiff and to cut true, which comes in handy for those important joinery cuts. I like a slightly larger saw known as a carcase saw because you get a bit more blade under the back and it can handle most of my joinery cutting needs.

Panel Saw

My saw has 14 ppi and, like my panel saw, is filed with a rip tooth designed to work well in rip and cross-grain cuts.

Coping Saw

This saw is essentially a small version of a bow saw that is suited for fine detail work like sawing inlays. In my shop, it primarily gets used for removing waste while dovetailing.

Nice Saws to have

Large Rip Saw and Crosscut Saw

A serious rip saw with 5 ppi is nice when you are breaking out lumber that is thicker than an inch. The bigger gullets carry out more waste and keep the cut straight and true. Just like an aggressive rip saw, a larger crosscut is helpful for thicker stock. An ideal tooth size would be 8 ppi filed with a crosscut shape.

Bow Saw

Bow saws or turning saws come in all shapes and sizes and are designed to cut curves. The blade is usually tensioned by cord and a winding peg that rests against the stretcher. The saw should have a narrow blade to allow cutting radii of almost any size.

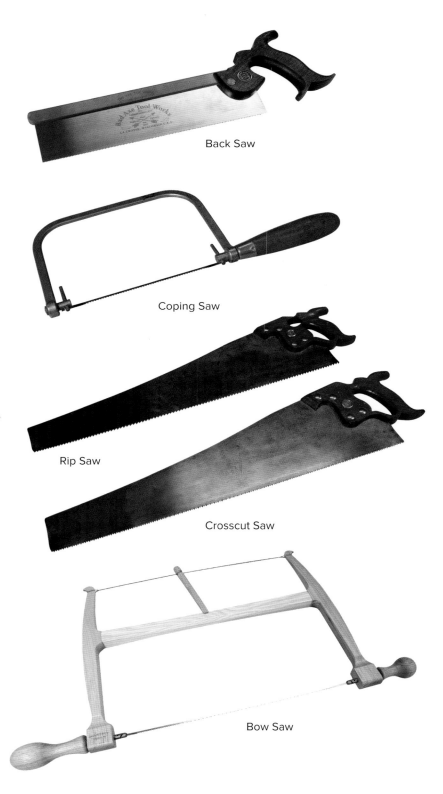

Back Saw

Coping Saw

Rip Saw

Crosscut Saw

Bow Saw

MARKING & MEASURING

There is a veritable hockey sock of marking and measuring tools on the market. The truth is some of these tools are more gadgetry than anything else. That being said, there are a few staples in this group of tools that no woodworker should be without.

Wheel Marking Gauge

I would be lost without wheel marking gauges. It is simply a fence with a rod that goes through it. At the end of the rod is a cutter wheel that incises the wood. The mark is easily found with an edge tool like a chisel. Imagine if you could put a chisel edge precisely on a pencil line anywhere. This is what a knife line made by a wheel marking gauge allows. It traps the chisel in exactly the spot the where you want it. I have four of these gauges

Compass

because I like to set different gauges up for different parts of a build. That way, if I mess something up I can easily re-mark a part and start over again.

Compass

Using a compass is the easiest way to draw a circle or parts of a circle. We are all familiar with this tool because we have been using them since grade school for various tasks. Personally, I like the ones that have a pencil holder as opposed to a piece of 2mm lead. I find that a pencil is easier to sharpen than those leads. Besides, being thrifty, I need to do something with those short pencils that are too small to hold comfortably in my hand.

Dividers

The divider is best described as a compass with two points. This tool is many millennia old and has been

Wheel Marking Gauges

used for many things like navigation, mathematics, and woodworking, to name a few. In my shop the divider is used primarily to lay out complicated geometry or to divide a board into equal parts, like in the case of dovetails or laying out shelf locations in a cabinet.

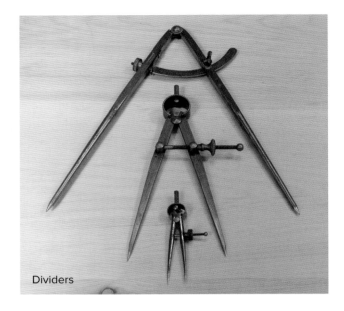

Dividers

Bevel Gauge

Angles are often used in woodworking but most times the actual number in degrees isn't needed. The bevel gauge has a reference head and a movable blade that can be set and used in conjunction with a pencil or knife to mark angles on the work. There are many designs of these tools out there but you'll want to look for a version that has a sturdy locking mechanism that doesn't interfere with the layout.

Bevel Gauges

12" Combination Square

This square has a reference head that has two surfaces: 90° and 45°, making it ideal for woodworking. The blade in the square is normally graduated and can be found in imperial and metric. There are other sizes of blades but I find this one to be the most useful for layout work.

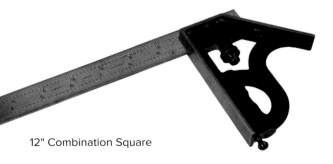

12" Combination Square

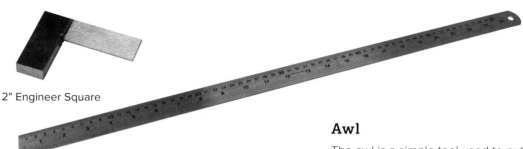

2" Engineer Square

24" Rule

2" Engineer Square

This little square is perfect to keep somewhere easily accessible like in an apron. Checking an edge for square is a task you'll do often. And you don't want to have to drag out the 12" combination square for this task every time.

24" Rule

A two-foot rule handles most of the measuring tasks for woodworking. On top of lay out work, a rule this size also comes in handy as a straight edge to guide pencils and knives.

Awl

The awl is a simple tool used to put a dimple on the surface of the wood to locate the exact location for drilling a hole or similar tasks.

Small Snap-Off-Blade Knife

These knives are indispensible in the shop. They are perfect for making light trimming cuts, cutting out paper patterns or veneer, and even sharpening pencils. You can also use them to mark joinery in a pinch. You can get them anywhere and at any price point but I like to spend a bit of money on these knives. The extra cash gives you better locking mechanisms and usually a better gripping surface. The snap-off blades make it easy to always keep a fresh edge; a dull knife is not good for anything.

Awl

Snap-Off-Blade Knife

Small Marking Knife

A good marking knife should have a single bevel, which allows you to keep the flat side against a straight edge or wooden component. These knives do the same job as the marking gauge. They cut a line into the wood to be used as a reference mark. My favorite type has a dual bevel because it can be used in any direction.

Pencils

I use a few different pencils in the shop. A carpenter's pencil is nice for gross marking and labeling of parts. I also use an H-lead pencil to accentuate a knife line. You simply drop the pencil into the knife line to fill it with lead. The hardness of the H pencil keeps it sharper longer so that it fits in the knife line easily. I don't like mechanical pencils because the lead is fragile. And because no one is perfect, invest in a quality eraser. A grease pencil is also handy for marking parts so that they are easy to spot on the bench.

Pencils and Erasers

Nice to Have

4" or 6" Adjustable Square

A smaller combination square is nice to have when it comes to laying out joinery. Sometimes using the 12" version is just too large for smaller surfaces.

Chalk Line

When marking boards to be ripped to rough width, I find a chalk line to be quite helpful. Be careful of the one you use in the wood shop. The ones commonly

6" Adjustable Square

Small Marking Knife

Chalk Line

seen for sale at home centers are fine for construction but they fall short for woodworking, in my opinion. Many of them send chalk flying everywhere when you pull out the cord, which gets all over you and the piece you are trying mark. The one pictured here is from Japan and has a small sponge in the tip of the chalk reservoir to remove any excess chalk. Sometime it's the little details that make all the difference in tool design.

BORING AND FASTENING
Brace and bits

A brace was what was used to drill holes before electric drills. Larger braces provide lots of power to drill holes and small ones are great for driving screws. The bits range in size from ¼" to 1" and are normally found in ¹⁄₁₆" increments. They are surprisingly simple tools and drilling accurately is easily learned with a bit of practice. The bits are auger style with a lead screw that draws the bit deeper in the hole as you turn the brace.

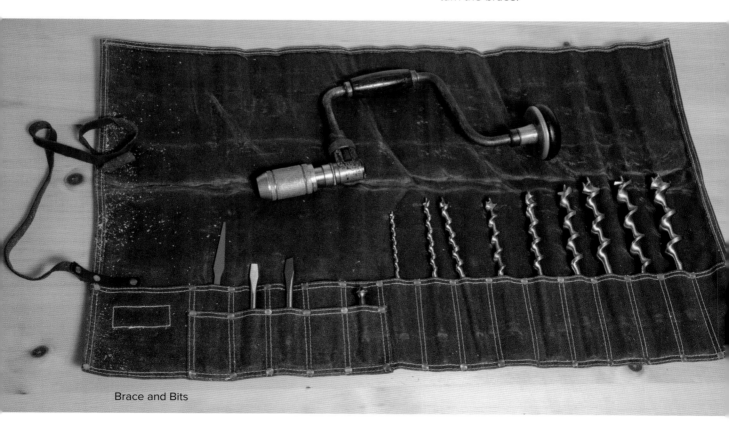

Brace and Bits

Eggbeater and Drills

For holes smaller than ¼", this eggbeater drill does the trick. You can also use the same drills that you use in a power drill. Brad point bits are ideal for woodworking because they cut cleanly. Find a set that ranges from 1⁄16" to ¼" in 1⁄64" increments. A set like this is perfect for drilling pilot holes for fasteners.

WORKSHOP WORKHORSES
Claw Hammer & Screwdrivers

Metal fasteners are a part of woodworking so a good claw hammer and screwdrivers are a must. I use Robertson and flat-head screws most so I have dedicated drivers for those; for the others I have a multi-driver.

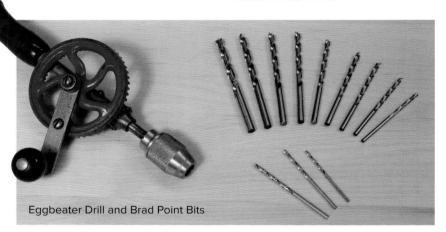

Eggbeater Drill and Brad Point Bits

Claw Hammer and Screwdrivers

Chisel Mallets

Chisels

Chisels

Chisels come in all shapes and styles, each one with a specific job in mind. To start, a set of bench chisels are all you'll need. They are available from home centers and specialty stores at price points that vary from $5 to $150 per chisel. My advice: pick the best you can afford. I've gotten a $5 chisel sharp but the edge retention was poor. With chisels, you get what you pay for.

Chisel Mallets

You're going to need something to hit your chisels with. Mallets come in many different shapes, sizes, and weights. What you strike your chisels with is a personal choice. Personally, I hit my chisels with a metal blacksmith's hammer and a brass mallet, depending on the work at hand. There is a lot of talk about metal damaging wooden handled chisels but I say bull pucky. I've been doing it for many years and haven't wrecked a single chisel. A wooden mallet would be my second choice, with plastic-faced hammers bringing up the rear. Ultimately you can strike your chisels with a rock; it's all about personal preference.

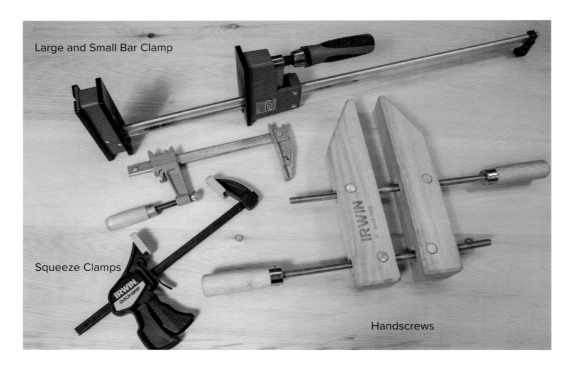

Large and Small Bar Clamp

Squeeze Clamps

Handscrews

Clamps

The old adage is true: You can't have too many clamps. But there are many different styles of clamps available and not all are created equal. I routinely use three types of clamps in my shop. I have other styles but they are mostly a variation of the main three that I use: bar clamps, squeeze clamps, and handscrews.

Shop Apron

Shop Apron

Regardless of how small your shop is, it's a good idea to wear a shop apron. I like them because they keep tools like a small square, pencils, wax, and many other things close at hand. You'd be surprised how easy it is to misplace a small square or pencil when the bench is covered in shavings. If you get into the habit of keeping these tools in an apron, you will never be caught searching for them. They also keep your clothes clean and give you handy place to remove glue from your fingers.

Machines

I'm not going to get too much into machines because there are already many books on the topic. I'm fortunate to have the space for a few machines in my shop but by no means do I 'need' them to woodwork. The focus of this book is working without them but if you have them feel free to bring them into the minimalist fold. Just make sure that they earn their keep in the shop. The box at right lists the machines that I run in my shop and how I use them. Depending on the kind of work you focus on, you may discover different power tools you'd prefer not to live without. Again, just make sure the tools you bring into your shop are worth the space they occupy.

POWER TOOLS: WHERE TO START?

Given the desire, space, and means, introducing power tools into your shop can certainly speed up a few tasks. If I had to choose just one it would be a bandsaw. Others argue convincingly that a lathe creates shapes that are almost impossible to replicate with only hand tools. Let the kind of work you do guide you in choosing the power tools you bring into your shop.

Bandsaw

- Ripping
- Re-sawing
- Cross-cutting
- Cutting curves
- Cutting tenons

Thickness planer

- Thicknessing boards

Drill press

- Drilling accurate holes
- Removing mortise waste quickly

Lathe

- Making furniture components like legs and pulls

Dust Collector

- Used to keep things clean when using messy power tools

Chapter 3

MARKING AND MEASURING TOOLS AND TECHNIQUES

One of the most important skills for a woodworker is to be able to measure and mark accurately. Without this foundational skill things are destined to go wrong. If your measuring is off or components are out of square, the imprecision will certainly surface in the finished project. The good news: Marking and measuring is actually pretty straightforward as long as you have a few basic tools and stick with simple, reliable techniques.

Measuring doesn't necessarily need to mean numbers. In fact, I rarely use numbers when I measure components because the numbers and fractions of numbers can cause confusion or errors due to poor math. There is nothing worse than trying to subtract $14\frac{23}{32}$ from $15\frac{7}{16}$. I know that this is simple math but why risk the error? So what's a woodworker to do? Use the referential measuring system that relies on marking out distances off the workpieces themselves rather than transferring measurements with a tape or rule. The process is much more simple and a lot less likely to introduce errors.

MEASURING

If I have a simple side table with a drawer in process in the shop and need to figure out the size of the drawer face, I could do some measurements, transpose them to the piece, and hope that I'm having a good day. Or, I could take a small stick called a story stick, place it in the opening for the drawer, and make two pencil marks on the stick that represent the size of the opening. Do I need to know what the actual numerical measurement is? Absolutely not! Stripping the numbers out of the process eliminates math or measurement errors.

USING A SQUARE

Squares have two main components to them: the reference head and the blade. The reference head is the part that gets put against the reference surface of a component. The blade gets used to gauge whether or not the adjacent surface is square to the reference surface.

To use the square correctly, place the head on the reference surface and slide it down the surface until the blade contacts the adjacent surface. If the whole blade is touching the surface then it is perpendicular (square) to the

reference surface. If it's not then that surface is out of square and you need to make adjustments. It's also important to keep the square straight on the board so you get an accurate reading. The same holds true for the 45° side of a combination square.

1 To check mating edges for squareness, begin by flushing the head of the square on one face of the stock.

2 While keeping the head of the square flush to the surface, slide it down so that the blade touches the mating face. Gaps between the face of the stock and the blade represent the degree to which your stock is out of square.

PENCIL LINE VS. KNIFE LINE

Woodworking mainly consists of removing material from wood, usually to a line of some sort. That being said, there are varying levels of accuracy required. If you are initially sawing out parts for a project, you leave them slightly oversized, which doesn't require a high level of accuracy. However, when bringing the same components to final dimension, you need to be as accurate as possible.

Pencils

In my shop, I typically use one of those flat lumber pencils for rough marking. When laying out a rough saw cut or labeling parts nothing beats it. As I said earlier, pencil marks are for coarse use, not for final dimensions or critical locating.

Lumber pencils are fairly soft, and you can easily use a pencil with HB lead for these tasks.

Marking Knives

When accuracy is important, I don't trust my marking to a pencil. Trimming boards to final dimension, marking joinery, or transferring critical locations get done with a marking knife. The advantage of the marking knife is that you have a physical location that you can slip a chisel into. A knife line is also used to create a saw groove to ensure an accurate cut. For those with more 'experienced' eyes, it's helpful to darken the knife line with a bit of pencil to make them easier to see. In this case, I recommend an H pencil because it will sharpen to a finer point and slip into the knife line easily.

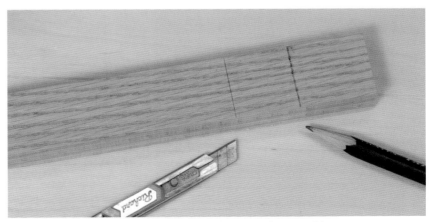

Knife marks are preferable to pencil lines because they provide a groove that helps you register your tools. Tracing the knife line with a pencil also makes it easy to see.

KNIFE MARKING TECHNIQUES

Pencils are pretty straightforward to use but a marking knife requires a bit of know-how. In order for knife lines to be effective they should be fairly deep (approximately ⅟₃₂"). What you don't want to do is try to hit that depth on the first strike. Put the knife in the location where you want your mark then bring the square blade up to the knife. Start off by creating a shallow knife mark and then progressively go deeper and deeper until you get to depth. If you're using a square or straight-edge as a guide, use light lateral pressure on the knife blade to be sure your line doesn't wander. Knives like to follow the grain so be mindful of the knife's location when you strike that initial light line.

1 To begin making a knife mark on stock, begin at the edge of the stock and allow your knife to bite securely into the wood.

2 Then slide your square against the knife and extend the knife line across the face of the stock.

MAKING A SAW GROOVE

Saw grooves have been in use for an awfully long time. They are one of the hidden secrets to accurate work with hand tools that disappeared when we all started using power tools. The saw groove is simply a small trench that goes across the grain that will accept a hand saw blade. This technique is what allows a woodworker to create a straight shoulder or an accurate trimming cut.

To start, make a knife line with a marking gauge or marking knife. Then use a chisel held at about 45° to remove a small amount of wood to create the groove. Then drop your saw right into the groove and start sawing. If your sawing is good you will have a nice shoulder or crosscut that will only need a bit of attention from a plane to finish it off.

1

2

3

1 A good saw groove makes it easier to register the blade of your hand tools exactly where you want it. Begin with a simple knife line.

2 Then work from the waste side of your mark and make small cuts with a chisel to create a trench.

3 The wide angled groove pushes the blade of your tool against the original knife line.

IDENTIFYING MARKS

There are many ways to mark your boards and components but I use two types of marks almost exclusively.

Face Side/Face Edge

It's important to know which face and which edge will be used to reference subsequent work like sizing and joinery. The easiest way is to use the two marks in the illustration to keep things straight.

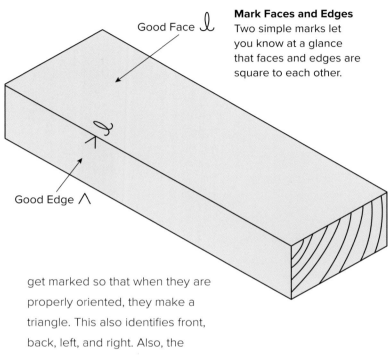

Good Face

Good Edge

Mark Faces and Edges
Two simple marks let you know at a glance that faces and edges are square to each other.

Cabinetmaker's Triangles

I've seen many marks and codes used to try to keep components labeled and oriented on people's benches. Words like inside, outside, top, bottom, left, right, fore, aft; and the list goes on. I've also seen various combinations of alphanumeric cyphers that look like you would need a codex to puzzle them out.

So forget all those crazy notions and embrace the cabinetmaker's triangle. This simple triangle marked on your components keeps your parts sorted and oriented. Take a look at the illustrations and you will see what I mean. The parts get marked so that when they are properly oriented, they make a triangle. This also identifies front, back, left, and right. Also, the outside of the triangle indicates the outside surface of the component. Conversely, the inside of the triangle indicates the inside surface.

This marking convention will work for any set of components from box parts to legs. If you have parts scattered all over your bench, you simply orient the components so that they make the triangle and you're good. I spend a lot of time picking the color and grain of wood to be as harmonious as possible; this marking system makes sure that I don't mess them up.

The Cabinetmaker's Triangle
Drawing a simple triangle that spans across the faces or edges of your stock is an easy way to keep parts correctly positioned throughout the building process.

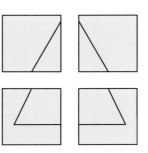

Tops of Four Legs

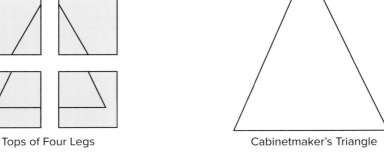

Cabinetmaker's Triangle

Left/Right

Top/Bottom

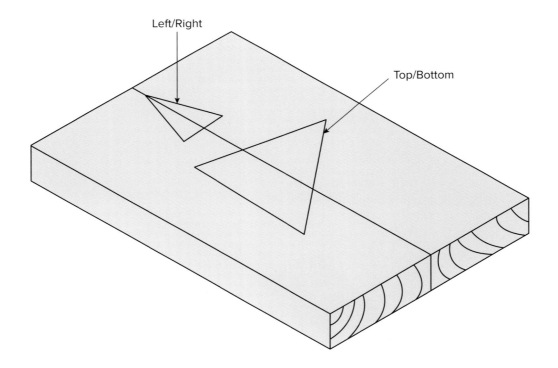

Chapter 4

PRACTICAL SHARPENING AND TOOL MAINTENANCE

There has been far too much ink spilled on the subject of sharpening. The woodworking forums are awash with the minutia of the topic but the fundamentals seem to get forgotten. It's actually very simple: Anything sharp has two flat and polished surfaces meeting at an edge. It doesn't matter how you get that edge—whether you use machines or water stones, jigs or no jigs—the goal is the same. Some folks drone on about sharpening so much that you forget that they are even a woodworker. I worry that they forget it too. My aim is simple: Get the tool sharp and get back to woodworking.

TERMINOLOGY

No matter what tool you're sharpening, the process can be broken into three basic categories.

Grinding — The first phase of sharpening create the geometry of the edge.

Honing — The second phase is used to refine the edge. For some tools like axes and planes used for rough work, you can stop at this point in the process.

Polishing — The final phase of sharpening that puts a keen edge on a tool for fine work and clean cutting.

Flat bevel — A flat bevel is achieved on some type of flat sharpening media like a stone, abrasive paper on glass, or a turntable-style power sharpener.

Hollow bevel — A concave bevel is created by a circular stone like those found on a wheel grinder.

Primary bevel angle — Think of the primary bevel as the starting point. When you have sharpened a tool many times or have damaged the edge, the primary bevel is where you return to start afresh. This gets created during the grinding phase of sharpening.

Secondary bevel angle — This is a small area at the edge of the blade that is a higher angle than the primary. The whole purpose of the secondary bevel is to reduce the amount of time it takes to hone and polish an edge.

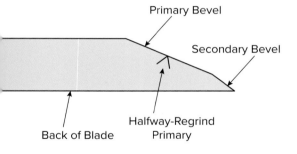

Primary Bevel

Secondary Bevel

Back of Blade

Halfway-Regrind Primary

Rounded Corners

Hard Corners

Light Camber

Heavy Camber

Plane Blade Shapes

ESTABLISH THE PRIMARY BEVEL

In my shop, I use a 6" bench grinder to establish the primary bevel because it is quick and efficient. If you don't own one of these tools then a coarse abrasive like a 220-grit stone will certainly do the trick. I grind all of my edges with a primary bevel of 25° so that I'm not changing the angle on my grinder's tool rest. Again, this assures that I'm getting the same geometry every time. I only grind a primary once my secondary bevel creeps up to past half way up the primary or if I've done damage to the edge that requires a lot of work to repair.

Outfitted with a quality wheel and a few accessories, a simple two-wheel grinder will tackle all of the jobs encounterd in a typical small shop.

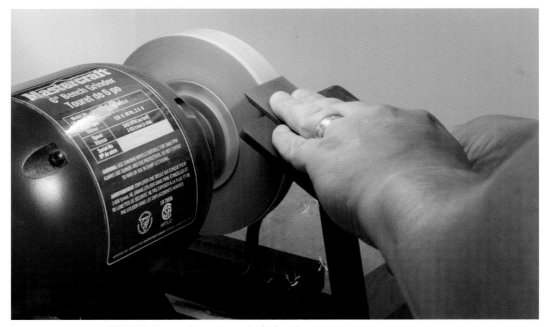

Invest in a high quality tool rest as the ones included with most grinders are completely inadequate. You need a stable rest that won't slip while you're establishing the bevel angle at the wheel.

FLATTEN THE BACK

Don't forget that a sharp edge is the result of two faces meeting at a point—and the back of the blade is just as important as the bevel. Once you establish the angle of the bevel at the grinder, use stones or your abrasive of choice to make sure the back of the blade is flat. Keep in mind that you don't need to flatten the entire back—only the last inch or so of the blade. Marking the end of the blade's back with a permanent marker makes it easy to determine when the blade is flat; once the markings are gone, the back is flat. I use a 3000-grit stone to do the initial flattening, then work up to as high as a 10,000-grit stone for the final polish.

Use a sharpening stone to flatten the lower inch or so of the blade. You'll know it's flat when there is a uniform scratch pattern across the width of the blade.

JIG OR NO JIG?

Another hotly debated issue is whether or not to use a sharping jig. Personally, I use a jig for most of my sharpening because it allows me to get repeatable results in a

short amount of time. This allows me to get back to woodworking with an edge that is predictable and reliable. I was taught how to sharpen by hand at school but I have abandoned this method because it's difficult to maintain the geometry of the edge. The angle of the edge typically creeps up as subsequent sharpening is done. I think hand sharpening is a romantic notion and a fact to brag about among its users but if you're like me and just want to get back to work, grab a jig and get on with it.

I've tried a few different methods of sharpening in my time and this is what I have settled on.

HONE AND POLISH THE SECONDARY BEVEL

For the honing and polishing phases I move over to my Japanese water stones and mount the blade in a jig. I normally mark the blades with the honing and polishing angle in permanent marker for easy reference. It takes about 30 seconds to place the blade in the jig then you are off to the stones. I use a 3000-grit stone to hone the secondary bevel then up to a 10,000 stone for the final polish. If you have sufficiently honed and polished the secondary you should feel a small burr on the back of the blade. All that's left is to remove that burr with a few strokes on your finest abrasive, remove the blade from the jig, and get back to work.

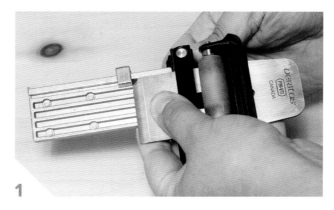

1

2

3

1 Begin the honing process by setting the blade in the jig and adjusting it to the desired bevel angle.

2 To hone the bevel, keep both the wheel of the jig and the bevel flat on the stone as you push and pull the blade back and forth on the stone.

3 After honing the bevel, flip the blade over and take just a few strokes across the stone to remove the burr.

THE SHARPENING BUCKET

My sharpening bucket makes it easy to work with water stones. Water stones are somewhat messy and it can be difficult to keep the water contained. The bucket is where I store my stones so they are always ready to go. I can easily flatten the stones by simply holding them above the bucket and dunking them in the water when needed. I built a bridge to sit on the bucket's rim so the stone has a place to rest while working. This bridge makes it easy to flush the stones with water without worrying about getting water everywhere. When the stones are not in use, the bridge comes off and the lid goes back on.

Mounting your waterstones over the top of a basic 5-gallon bucket keeps your bench and shop from becoming a wet mess.

The front and back of the wooden bridge is outfitted with simple wooden feet to seucure it in place. Rubber attached to the bridge steadies the stone.

TAKE A MINUTE FOR MAINTENANCE

Chislels are pretty straightforward. And while still simple tools, planes do have a few moving parts that should stay in good working order. When you have your plane apart for sharpening, you might as well do some maintenance. It's much better to do a minute of preventative maintenance than an hour of corrective maintenance. I do this every time I sharpen to ensure that I'm not getting sidelined.

- Remove surface rust on bare metal surfaces and apply oil
- Remove sawdust and dirt from the inside of the plane
- Clean and oil any adjusters
- Check the body for any nicks on the edges and remove them

It only takes a minute or so but your tools will thank you for it. Now that your tools are in order, it's time for the fun part. Let's start woodworking.

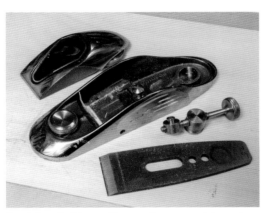

Don't be afraid to pull your planes apart to make sure they stay in good working order.

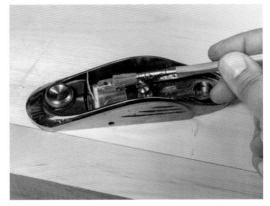

A small brush comes in handy for sweeping away shavings and debris that build up as you work.

Add a drop of oil to the blade aduster and any other moving parts.

A few drops of oil keep any threaded parts operating smoothly.

THE MINIMALIST WOODWORKER
A CHECKLIST

Workspace:

Only the basics are required. In as little as 40 square feet you can be up and running. Look for or provide only a few essentials:

- **Power:** If you rely mostly on handtools, providing power for lighting is your main concern.
- **Flooring:** Look for something forgiving on your feet and dropped tools.
- **Heating/Cooling:** Necessary only if you're in an unheated area or a damp basement that needs some help drying out.
- **Basic Toolset:** Buy only what you'll use and remember that less is often more.

Sharpening:

A sharp edge is nothing more than two faces that come together at a point. There are myriad ways to achieve that point, but a few basics will do the trick:

- Grinder
- Waterstones
- Honing jig
- 5-Gallon bucket

THE MINIMALIST'S TOOLSET

Planes

- Jack Plane
- Shoulder Plane
- Plow Plane
- Router Plane

Saws

- Panel Saw
- Back Saw
- Coping Saw

Marking & Measuring

- Wheel Marking Gauge
- Compass
- Dividers
- Bevel Gauge
- 12" Combination Square
- 24" Rule
- 2" Engineer's Square
- Awl
- Small Snap-off Blade Knife
- Pencils

Drilling:

- Brace
- Auger Bits
- Egg-beater Drill
- Brad-point drill bits

Other:

- Clawhammer
- Screwdrivers
- Chisels
- Chisel Mallets
- Clamps
- Shop Apron

Nice to have:

- Jointer Plane
- Smoothing Plane
- Block Plane
- Rabbet Plane
- Large Rip Saw
- Large Crosscut Saw
- 4" or 6" Aadjustable Square
- Chalk Line

Chapter 5

SAW BENCH
AND BENT

Building a saw bench and bent is a good way to start equipping your minimalist shop. Then bench comes in handy for sawing and countless other tasks. The bent adds extra versatility to the bench, allowing you to support long boards. This bent is also designed so that it can be nested in the bench for storage so that it's not in the way.

It's not only sawing that will be made a joy with this bench. It makes a great assembly surface, it's the perfect height for drilling with a brace, and it's even a great place to take a load off and think. The joinery for this project is fairly simple but you will learn a lot in the process of building it.

So what is a bent? The word bent comes from the timber framing world. A bent is a framework composed of several structural members that defines the cross-section of a timber frame building or supports a trestle. Put simply, a bent is a movable saw horse that is the same height as the saw bench. It allows you to support longer boards for sawing at the bench.

TOOLS

back saw
rip panel saw
flush-cut saw
coping saw
jack plane
smoother
shoulder plane
marking gauge
compass
ruler
brace and bits
chisels
mallet
screw driver

MATERIALS

clear pine
painter's or masking tape
#8 1½" screws
PVA glue

CUT LIST—SAW BENCH (FROM 1 X 12 X 8')

PART	QUANTITY	THICKNESS	WIDTH	LENGTH
Top	2	¾"	5½"	24"
Sides	2	¾"	10½"	19¼"
Stretchers	4	¾"	3"	22"

CUT LIST—BENT (FROM 1 X 6 X 6')

PART	QUANTITY	THICKNESS	WIDTH	LENGTH
Foot	2	¾"	2½"	12"
Top Stretcher	1	¾"	2½"	22"
Lower Stretcher	1	¾"	2½"	20½"
Upright	2	¾"	2½"	18"

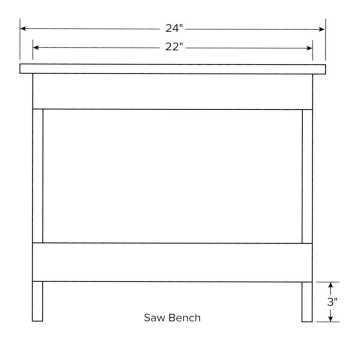

Saw Bench

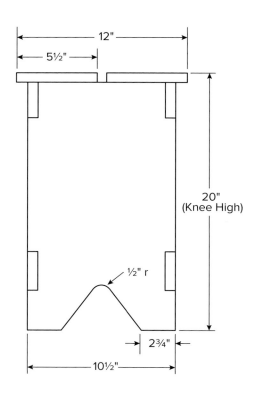

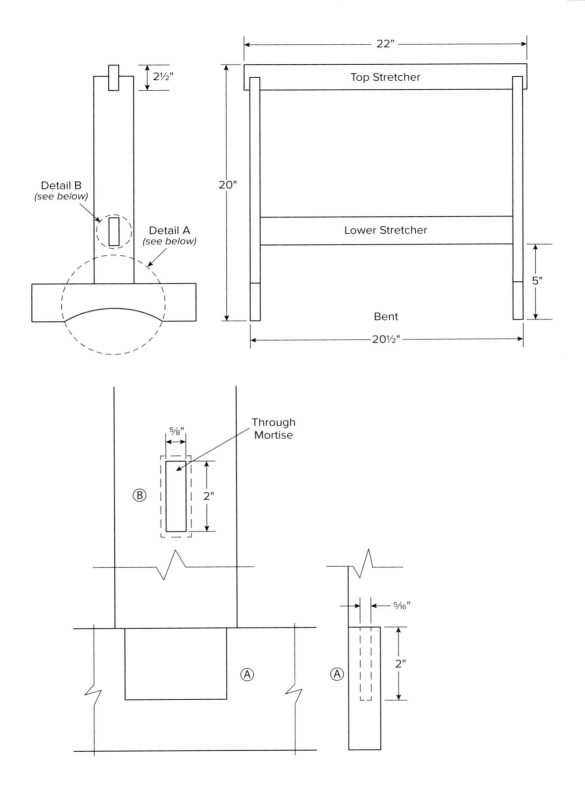

Saw Bench

PLAN OUT THE PARTS

1 Mark out all of your components on the 1 x 12 and start by breaking out the large board into smaller, easier-to-handle pieces. To begin laying out the parts, mark the lenght of the two sides across the full width of the 1 x 12.

2 Mark off the tops by dividing the width in half using the ruler. Then mark out the stretchers, dividing into four equal parts using a ruler. Note that you can angle the ruler across the stock, then find the centerlines—it's an easy way to simplify the math.

3 Be sure to label each part so you can tell at a glance where each part belongs.

CUT OUT ALL THE COMPONENTS

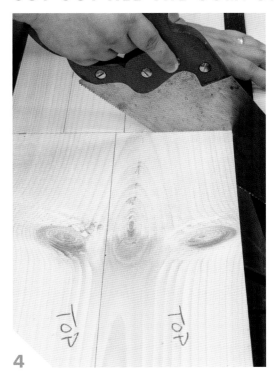

4

5

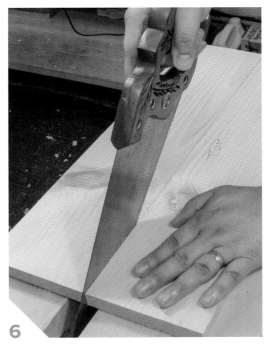

6

4 Make all of the crosscuts first so that the long unwieldy stock is easier to handle.

5 Joint one edge of each part before you rip to them to width. A jack plane works well for this task.

6 Work on a flat surface to rip the stock along its length.

CUT OUT ALL THE COMPONENTS, *continued*

7

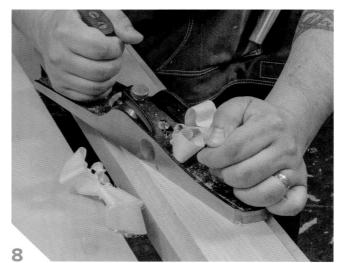

8

7 As you saw, the stock may have a tendency to close up after the saw passes through it. Place a wedge in the kerf to keep it from closing on the saw.

8 Use a jack or smoothing plane to surface all of the components and remove the saw marks.

9 Mark mating components using cabinetmaker's triangles to help keep the parts in order as you work.

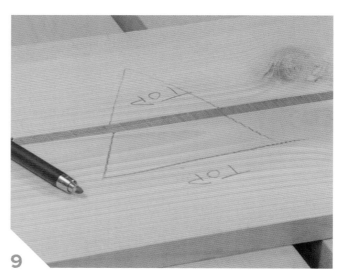

9

10 Mark the final length on the parts using the marking knife and square.

11 Chisel out a saw groove to create a trench for you to drop the saw into.

12 Saw off the waste, being sure to keep the saw plate perpendicular to the face of the stock.

10

11

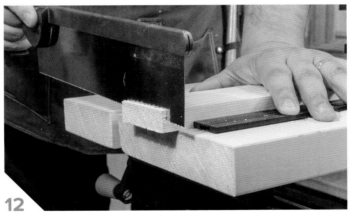

12

WHAT IS A SAW GROOVE?

Essentially, a saw groove is exactly what it sounds like: a small groove that you can lay a saw into to ensure that you are cutting exactly where you want to. The saw groove also gives you a clean shoulder to work with, which is essential to crisp-looking joinery.

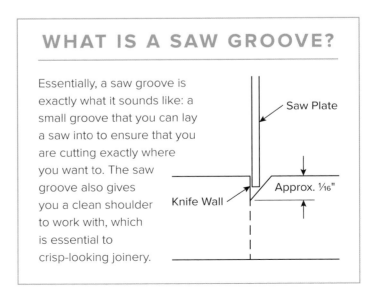

MARK THE JOINERY ON THE SIDES

13 Use the actual stretchers to mark out their width on the three sides. Use a marking knife and go over the mark with a pencil to make it easier to see.

14 Set the marking gauge to match the thickness of your stretcher.

15 Mark out the thickness of the stretcher on the stock used for the sides.

16

17

16 Gauge lines for the thickness on both sides and connect the lines to the edge with a square and a marking knife.

17 Mark your waste with a pencil to remind you to saw on the correct side of the line.

MARK OUT EVERYTHING FIRST

Be sure to mark all of the joinery before starting to cut it out. This will make the layout phase go smoother and you won't have to worry about missing chunks of wood as you're trying to use a square.

MARK THE SIDE CUTOUTS

18

18 Mark the centerline on the bottom edge of the sides. Then set your square to the width of the stretcher. Draw a horizontal line at this distance up along the centerline. Then draw a pencil line the width of the stretcher from both edges of the sides.

19 Draw the upper half of a ¾" circle at this intersection using a compass.

20 Connect the mark at bottom of the sides with the tangent of the circle.

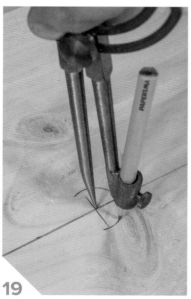

19

20

CUT THE TOP STRETCHER NOTCHES

21 Cross-cut to the depth of the notches in the sides using a back saw.

22 Secure the stock and use a panel saw to rip cut the remainder of the notch to create the joint.

23 Once the notch is cut, the excess stock falls away.

24 At this stage you can use a chisel to make adjustments if necessary. Make long paring cuts to refine the joint to the lines.

CUT THE BOTTOM STRETCHER NOTCHES

25 Cross-cut to depth to create the shoulders with a back saw. Then remove the bulk of the waste using a coping saw. As you cut, leave the knife line and plan to refine the notch later.

26 With the stock flat on your work surface, begin to chisel to the line. Work slowly to prevent cutting beyond the marked lines.

27 Work to the center then come in from the other side to ensure clean lines.

28 The finished notches should be pared smooth with a chisel.

25

26

27

28

CUT THE BOTTOM DECORATIVE DETAIL

29

29 Mark the hole location with an awl.

30 Drill a ¾" through hole with a brace and ¾" bit.

31 Saw on the lines to remove the waste. I find it easiest to tilt the board, making the cut line vertical.

32 Clean up the saw cuts with a file if necessary.

30

31

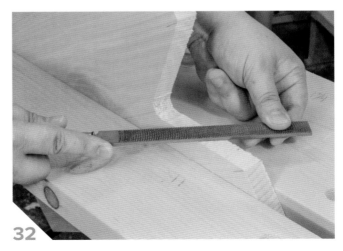

32

ASSEMBLE THE STRETCHERS AND ATTACH THE TOP

33

34

33 Attach the bottom and top stretchers to the first side without glue and drill ⅛" pilot holes for the screws. Then add glue to the joint, reposition the stretchers and screw them into place. Repeat for the second side.

34 Mark the center on the top of each side. Mark ½" on either side of the centerline. Ensure that the overhang is equal on the ends. Once satisfied with the position, drill pilot holes and fasten with screws. Don't glue the top to the base—this makes it easier to replace when it becomes worn from work.

Bent

PREPARE ALL PARTS AND MORTISE THE FEET

1 Mark out all components on the 1 x 6. Then cross-cut, rip, and plane all of the parts to final dimensions. Focus on the feet next. Mark out the top and bottom of the $5/16$" x 2" mortises in the center of each foot using a marking knife and a square.

2 Establish the width of the mortise using a marking gauge. Marking from each face ensures that the mortise is centered on the stock.

3 Attaching a painter's or masking tape flag is an easy way to create a depth indicator on the bit. Drill out waste using a ¼" auger bit.

4 Pare out the remaining waste with a chisel to your layout lines. After paring to the bottom of the mortise, square up the ends and your mortise is complete.

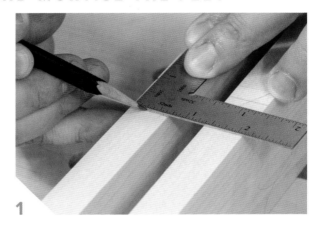

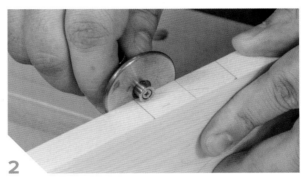

MARK OUT TENONS ON THE UPRIGHTS

5

6

7

8

9

5 Find the depth of the mortise with a double square or ruler.

6 Set a marking gauge ¹⁄₁₆" short of this length. Setting it just a bit short ensures that the tenon won't bottom out in the mortise, hanging up the joint during assembly.

7 Mark the shoulders using a marking gauge.

8 Cutting in a saw groove helps ensure accuracy.

9 Set another marking gauge for the cheeks. At this stage, mark them just a bit oversized. You can pare them for a perfect fit in a later step.

CUT TENONS ON THE UPRIGHTS

10 Begin to form the tenon by first cutting the shoulders.

11 Secure the work upright and rip the cheeks.

12 Test and tune the fit. Use a shoulder plane to pare down the tenon thickness until it slides into the mortise with moderate hand pressure.

13 Be mindful of taking equal amounts of material off each side so the tenon remains centered.

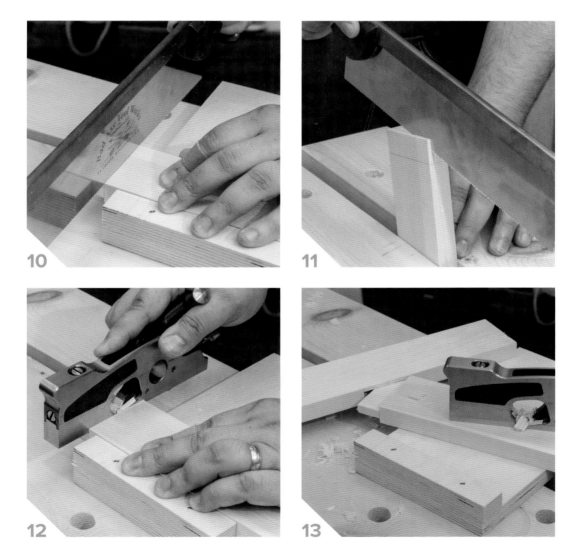

CUT TENONS ON THE UPRIGHTS, *continued*

14 To mark out the short shoulders, center the tenon on the mortise board and transfer the width onto the tenon.

15 Carry the lines down with a square and make a short rip cut down to the shoulder of the tenon.

16 Reposition the stock and cut the shoulder line. Then double-check the fit of the joint and adjust as necessary.

14

15

16

MARK AND CUT THROUGH MORTISES
FOR THE LOWER STRETCHER

17 Measure up 3" from the
bottom tenon shoulder
and strike a line across
the upright. Then aline the
stretcher with this line and
use its width to set the length
of your mortise.

18 Find the center of the upright
width and strike a line.

19 Strike two lines on either side
of the centerline to create a
$\frac{5}{16}$" mortise.

17

18

19

MARK AND CUT THROUGH MORTISES
FOR THE LOWER STRETCHER, *continued*

20

21

22

20 Carry the lines around to the other side and mark the mortise on the opposite side of the upright.

21 Drill out the majority of the waste with a ¼" brace bit. Be sure to place a waste board under the upright so that the hole doesn't blow out the grain on the bottom side.

22 Pare to the knife lines with a chisel from both ends to avoid blowing out the grain.

MARK AND CUT TENONS ON THE LOWER STRETCHER

23

24

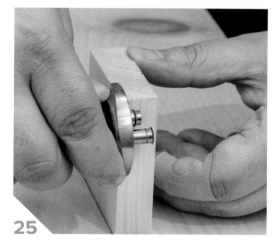

25

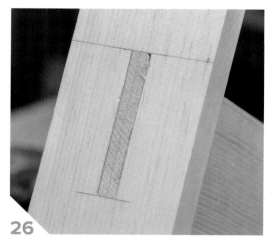

26

23 Set your marking gauge to the thickness of the ends of the bent.

24 Transfer this measurement to the ends of the stretcher stock. The tenons are left long and trimmed after assembly. See the Bent Details drawing on page 63 for the details.

25 Use a marking gauge to mark the thickness of the tenon. You can make two passes with a single-blade marking gauge or use a double-blade gauge, as shown here.

26 Saw out the tenon as you've done on earlier parts, using a knife wall to help ensure accuracy. Once complete, test fit and tune the joint like you did with the previous mortise and tenon joints.

MARK AND CUT THE NOTCHES ON THE TOPS OF THE UPRIGHTS

27 Mark out the thickness of the stretcher by marking directly off the actual part. Line the mating parts up to centerlines drawn on each.

28 Mark out the depth of the notch using a marking gauge.

29 Begin to cut the notch by sawing down to the baseline.

27

28

29

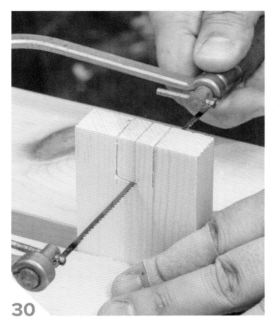

30

31

30 Use a coping saw to cut just shy of the baseline of the notch.

31 Clean up the bottom of the notch with a few taps on your chisel.

32 Test fit the joint and make adjustments as necessary.

32

MARK THE CURVE ON THE FOOT

33 To begin marking the shape of the foot, mark 1" from the ends of the foot.

34 Mark the center of the foot, then make a mark ½" up on the centerline.

35 Arch the drawing bow or a thin length of stock to line up with all three marks and pencil in the curve.

36 The finished shape is a smooth arc.

33

34

35

36

CUT OUT THE CURVE

37

37 Create a number of relief cuts by cross-cutting down to the line approximately every ½" with a back saw.

38 Using a 1" chisel with the bevel facing down, begin wasting out the curve by striking the chisel with a mallet.

39 Start from the ends and work into the center to reduce the chance of tearing out.

38

39

CUT OUT THE CURVE, *continued*

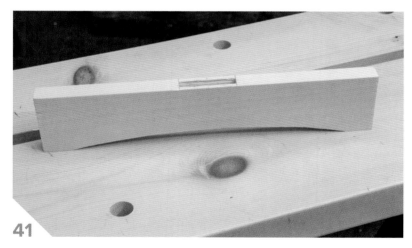

40 Once the bulk of the waste is removed, use the same chisel guided with hand pressure to pare to the line, creating a fair curve.

41 The finished foot is not only pleasing to the eye, it also helps stabilize the bent when working on uneven surfaces.

PREPARE AND ASSEMBLE THE ENDS

42 Dry assemble the feet, uprights, and lower stretcher then tune and fit the top stretcher. Once satisfied with the fit, use a smoothing plane to smooth all surfaces. You're just looking to get rid of pencil marks and road dirt so have the plane set to take the finest of shavings.

43 Begin final assembly of the ends by adding glue to the mortises on the feet. Slide the tenon into the mortise and close up the joint with a clamp

44 A single clamp is all that is required to glue up an end. Once clamped down, allow at least 2 hours for the glue to set.

BRING THE ENDS TOGETHER

45 Add glue to both the mortises on the ends and the tenons on the stretcher.

46 Clamp the lower stretcher to the uprights, taking care to see that the two ends remain parallel after the clamps are tightened.

47 After the assembly dries, add glue to the notches at the top of each end.

45

46

47

HARD-WON WISDOM

Getting glue squeeze-out can be a challenge. If you try to remove it too early the liquid glue will just get pushed around the area, contaminating the surrounding wood. Wait too long, and the hardened glue will tear-out wood fibers when you try to remove it. Ideally, you want to remove the glue when it becomes rubbery. Usually the glue hits this state in about 30 to 60 minutes.

48 Add a couple of clamps to secure the top of the bent in place.

49 Once the glue is dry, trim the ends of the protruding tenons using a flush cut saw, if available. Otherwise, simply saw as close as you can and clean up the endgrain with a chisel.

50 Then take light passes with a plane to smooth the surfaces.

51 Nest the bent with the saw bench and plane material off the top stretcher until it is level with the bench.

USING THE BENCH AND BENT

The saw bench and bent will be real workhorses in your shop and will be around for many years. Don't worry too much about dings, scratches, and scars . . . it just means that you're working.

RIPPING ON A SAW BENCH

The bench is pretty self-explanatory. Simply place a board to be cut on the bench and start sawing. To use the ripping groove for rip cuts, start the cut off the bench then move inboard with the saw in the groove and keep sawing. Be sure to move the board forward as you cut so you don't cut through the end of your saw bench. For longer boards, slide the bent as far out as it needs to be to support your work piece.

1

2

3

1 Steady the work with your knee and bodyweight, and start the cut with the stock hanging off the saw bench.

2 For long ripping cuts, position the cut in the void at the center of the saw bench.

3 When you're ready to cross-cut, longer stock can be stabalized on the saw bent.

ADD HOLES FOR BENCH ACCESSORIES

You can drill holes in the top of your saw bench to use the many bench accessories available at retailers or shop-made ones too. They certainly aren't necessary but they definitely make some tasks easier.

A SIMPLE FENCE IS LIKE AN EXTRA HAND

Adding a simple fence to one side of the bench allows you to push your work up against it to provide extra support as you work.

Chapter 6

SHOOTING BOARD HOOK

The key to getting the most out of any work bench is having effective ways to hold work to it. I'm not talking about vises here; I'm talking about bench appliances that make common tasks with hand tools much easier. This one jig has many uses and combines two often-used tasks: cross-cutting with a saw and truing up that cut with a plane. Once you see how this appliance works you will wonder how you got along without it.

The design inspiration for this board comes from the British magazine *The Woodworker* published in 1939. The neat features of this design are the ability to adjust the fence when it becomes worn or to remove it completely to shoot long grain. This model harkens back to a day when they were made of solid wood rather than modern sheet goods. If you are sinister (left-handed), you can easily reverse the runner and foot to make it perfect for a southpaw. More on the uses and techniques a bit later.

The fence holds the work in place while you cross-cut, then you can simply slide the piece over and shoot the edge with a plane lying on its side. It's not always easy to saw perfectly square in two directions. With this appliance, you can get close with the saw and then tune up the cut with a couple quick passes with a plane.

As for the plane to use, you will want to use one that has an effective cutting angle of about 40°. This slightly lower angle will make severing end-grain much easier. This isn't to say that you need a speciality plane. Most bevel-up style planes will be able to achieve this cutting angle easily.

This is a fairly simple build but it's important to follow the steps in order to have things work out right. Let's get building.

TOOLS

pencil
ruler
rip panel saw
jack plane
glue spreader
clamps
chisels
mallet
break-off knife
back saw
router plane
square
brace and bit
brush
screwdriver

MATERIALS

pine or other stock
#8 1¼" screws
PVA glue

CUT LIST

PART	THICKNESS	WIDTH	LENGTH
Deck	¾"	8"	16"
Fence	1¼"	2"	8"
Runner	½"	6"	16"
Foot	½"	2"	16"
Cleat	½"	½"	11"

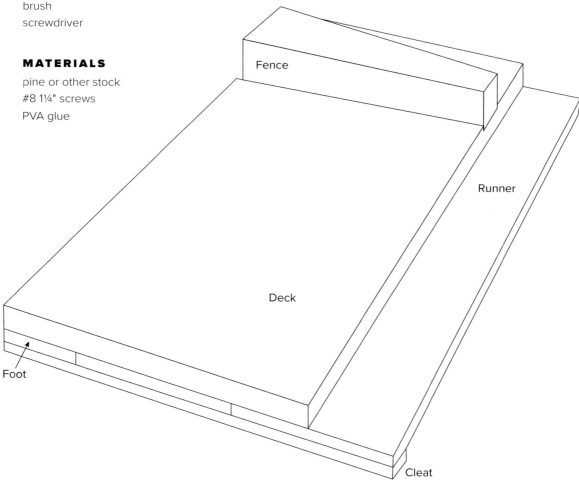

BUILD THE DECK AND FENCE

1 Begin by cutting all the parts from the cut list to size. Then flatten and a face and edge on each. Once they're brought to final dimension, laminate two ¾" thick pieces to create the fence. Begin by spreading an even layer of glue on the two mating faces.

2 Use a few clamps to bring the two surfaces together. Seeing a bead of glue squeeze out on all of the edges lets you know you have good glue coverage.

BUILD THE DECK AND FENCE, *continued*

3

4

3 Once the glue dries, mark the angle of the fence using a ruler. Set it at the corner of one end and the midpoint of the other end. Using a white pencil on dark woods makes it easy to see.

4 Saw and then plane the angled face of the fence so that it feels smooth underhand.

MAKE THE DADO

5 Strike a line square to the right edge of the deck.

6 Place a wide chisel into the knife line and place the fence's straight edge against the chisel.

7 Hold the fence down so it doesn't move and remove the chisel. Strike a line along the tapered edge of the fence without moving it. The tapered edge should be at the top of the deck.

5

6

7

MAKE THE DADO, *continued*

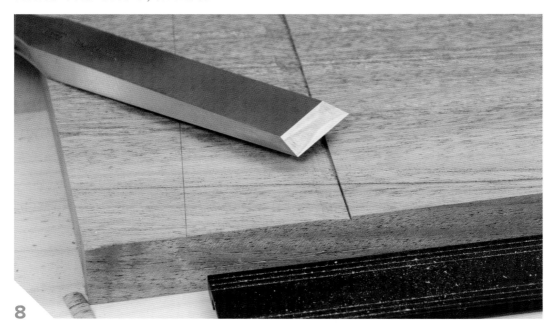

8

9

10

8 Creating saw grooves on both knife lines outlining the cutout
for the fence makes it easy to register your saw when it comes
time to cut the dado.

9 Set your marking gauge to about ¾6" and mark a line denoting
the depth of the dado used to house the fence.

10 Set the blade of your back saw in the saw groove and saw
down to the depth line.

11 Hog out the majority of the waste with a chisel held bevel-down for maximum control.

12 Finalize the depth using a router plane.

13 Careful work with a router plane creates a dado that is smooth, allowing your fence to slide easily in place.

ADD THE FENCE

14 Lightly tap the fence into the tapered slot and trim the fence to be almost flush with the edge of the deck. Confirm that the fence is square.

15 Plane a small (⅛") chamfer on the bottom of the deck for dust clearance.

16 Also chamfer the edges of the dado so they don't fracture when you take the fence on and off.

14

15

16

MAKE THE RUNNER AND FOOT

17 Mark the location of the runner on the underside of the deck as per the drawing. Clamp in place temporarily to drill the pilot holes.

18 Use a brace and bit to pre-drill ⅛" screw holes to secure the runner to the deck.

19 Attach the runner with glue and screws. Attach the foot using the same technique as the runner.

17

18

19

MAKE THE RUNNER AND FOOT, *continued*

20 Adding a few screws through the runner and into the deck secures everything in place.

21 Attach the cleat to the runner and foot with glue and a couple of screws.

22 Use a plane on its edge to bring the fence flush with the deck.

INSTRUCTIONS FOR USE

Traditionally this board would be used for shooting alone but in the interest of reducing clutter at the bench, I use mine as a bench hook for sawing as well. Bench hooks and shooting boards often get used in tandem and there isn't much difference in the appearance and functionality of the two, so why not, eh?

SAWING

Like the saw bench, the board is pretty intuitive to use. Simply put the part you want to cut against the fence and cross-cut to your heart's content. Just be mindful to not cut into the fence—extend the part just past the fence.

SHOOTING

After cross-cutting comes a quick trim called shooting. Place your plane on the runner and take a few passes to correct any errant sawing, leaving the end perfectly planed and square.

WORKING THE LONG GRAIN

To shoot the long-grain surface of a component, remove the fence with a couple of light mallet blows and place the part on the deck. The edge being shot only needs to extend over the deck by about a ¹⁄₁₆". Run the plane along the edge to get a straight perpendicular edge.

Sawing

Shooting

Working the Long Grain

HARD-WON WISDOM

When shooting with a plane, you want to make sure that the sides are perpendicular to the sole. Any deviation from square here will be transferred to the pieces you are planing.

Chapter 7

WOODEN MALLET

One of my favorite things to do in woodworking is to make my own tools. There is an undeniable feeling of satisfaction when you create a custom tool that fits your hand just right and does the job it was designed to do.

A wooden mallet is one of the easier tools to make and also one of the most useful. This mallet has two different faces to handle all the hitting tasks you will ask of it. One face is the plain end grain, which is perfectly suited to hitting chisels or setting holdfasts on the bench. The end grain is plenty tough and will stand up to repeated pounding.

The second face is covered with leather for tasks that require a little more finesse. When guiding joints together, sometimes you need a little persuasion to get them fully home. While you want to deliver a solid hit, you don't want to damage the smoothed surfaces with a mallet strike. You won't want this mallet to stray too far from your hand and you may be surprised how often you reach for this shop-made tool.

This mallet is made from tougher stuff than pine—red oak. A pine mallet would not have the weight and durability that you'll be asking of this tool.

TOOLS

pencil
ruler
panel saw
jack plane
smoothing plane
marking knife
marking gauge
chisels
mallet
router plane
clamps
back saw
spokeshave
grease pencil
utility knife
low-angle plane

MATERIALS

red oak
glue
sand
leather
water-based
contact cement
boiled linseed oil

CUT LIST

PART	QUANTITY	THICKNESS	WIDTH	LENGTH
Head	2	1⅜"	2⅞"	5"
Handle	1	¾"	1¾"	12¼"
Leather	1	3⁄16"	3"	3 ½"

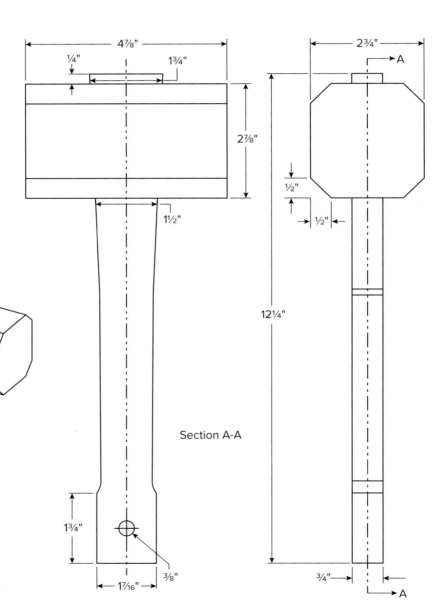

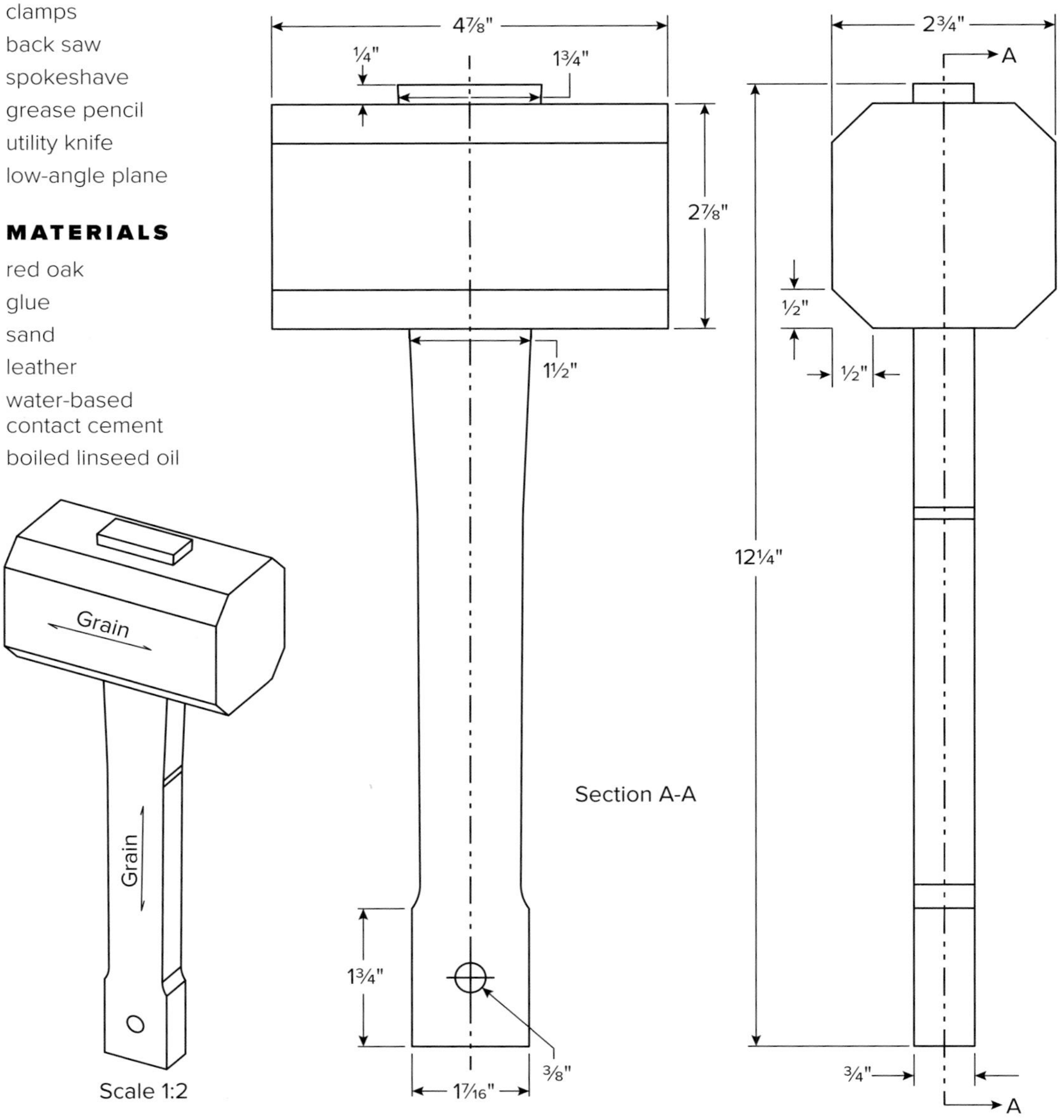

Section A-A

Scale 1:2

BREAKOUT YOUR PARTS

1 Begin by laying out the handle of your mallet on your plank, paying attention to the grain direction. Mark the top of the handle 1¾" from the edge, according to the drawing on page 106. Then mark the bottom of the handle 1⁷⁄₁₆" from the edge. Connect the two marks to create the taper.

2 Clamp up the handle and saw it out from the plank using a panel saw.

3 Use a jack or smoothing plane to smooth and refine all four sides of the handle.

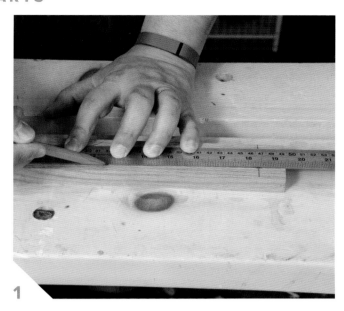

1

3

2

PREPARE THE MALLET HEAD

4 Mark and saw the stock you'll use to make up the mallet head. Then smooth the inside faces of the parts using a smoothing plane.

5 Mark out the center of the head parts by drawing in diagonals and a vertical centerline.

6 On the inside faces of the mallet head, mark out the width of the dado that will accept the mallet handle. To make sure your marks are precise, hold the mallet handle in place and mark directly off its profile using a marking knife.

4

5

6

7 On the stock that makes up the top of the mallet head, mark a cabinetmaker's triangle to help keep parts aligned throughout assembly. Then extend the dado lines across the top and bottom faces of the mallet head.

8 Set a marking gauge to half that of the handle's thickness (⅜") and strike your depth lines on the top and bottom of the mallet head.

9 Use a wide chisel to establish the shoulder. Alternate by chopping straight down and then in toward the shoulder line. Continue making the shoulders deeper with every set of cuts until you get close to the depth lines.

7

8

9

PREPARE THE MALLET HEAD, *continued*

10 Establish the mating shoulder line and remove excess stock in the same way, until you're left with only a small mountain of stock to remove from the center.

11 Once the two shoulders are established, use a wide chisel to quickly remove the bulk of the remaining waste.

12 Set your router plane to the final depth and remove the last bit of waste. In a ring-porous wood like oak, be sure to work the dado from both sides so you don't blow the grain out.

Test fit the handle to ensure that the dado's shoulders are equal. Check to be sure that the two head pieces will meet with the handle installed. If the handle is too thick, simply remove some material with a hand plane.

10

11

12

GLUE UP THE HEAD

13 Spread glue on the two inside surfaces, avoiding the dados. You can sprinkle a few grains of sand into the glue to prevent the two pieces from slipping around when you clamp them.

14 Place the handle into one half and place the second half on top. You are using the handle as a registration guide to ensure the correct position of the head pieces. Use the handle to register the two halves then clamp the assembly with 'F' clamps.

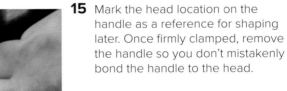

15 Mark the head location on the handle as a reference for shaping later. Once firmly clamped, remove the handle so you don't mistakenly bond the handle to the head.

Once the glue becomes rubbery, clean any squeeze-out in the mortise with a chisel.

WHILE THE HEAD IS DRYING

16 Mark a line 1" below the location where the bottom of the mallet head will sit on the handle. Then measure 1¾" from the bottom of the handle and ¼" from the sides. Connect the two points with a pencil line.

17 Make a series of crosscuts to the lines with a back saw.

18 Remove the waste from the sides of the handle using long paring cuts with a chisel.

19 Shape the pommel to your satisfaction. Chamfer both the top and bottom of the handle using a chisel.

20 Create the final shape with a spokeshave and remove hard corners, making sure that the handle is comfortable in the hand.

16

17

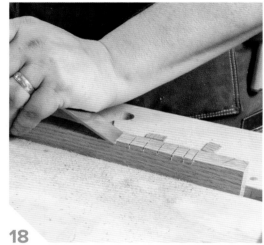

18

19

20

FINAL SHAPING

21 Smooth all four sides of the mallet head using a smoothing plane.

22 Mark the width of the chamfers on the head using a marking gauge set to about ⅛". You can darken the lines with pencil lead to make them easier to see.

23 Plane the chamfers into the mallet head and give the whole head a final smoothing.

24 Don't forget to smooth the end-grain of the mallet head as well.

25 Slide the handle in place and trim the top so that only about ¼" is protruding from the top of the mallet head.

21

22

23

24

25

APPLY LEATHER AND ADD A FINISH

26 Trace out the shape of the mallet head on the leather.

27 Trim the leather to size using a utility knife or other sharp blade. It's okay to trim it slightly oversized at this point.

28 Attach the piece of leather to one of the faces using water-based contact cement. Follow the instructions on the can—most require laying on a coat of cement to each of the mating surfaces.

29 Lay the leather on your bench and press the head of the mallet onto it. With most contact cement, only a few seconds of pressure are required.

26

27

28

29

30 Trim the leather to size using a utility knife or other sharp blade.

31 Once it is attached, use a utility knife to trim the leather to the final shape and size. Finally, ease the corners of the leather using a low-angle plane to finish things off.

32 The mallet doesn't need much in the way of finish. A few coats of boiled linseed oil should do it. Just be careful with those oily rags—they can auto-combust if left in bundles on your bench or floor.

Chapter 8

WORKBENCH

There isn't a tool in the shop that is more important than a workbench. When you bring the tools to the work, it's essential that the surface you work on is sturdy and flat. You also need the ability to secure work to the top of the bench to allow frustration-free work.

The workbench in this chapter is inspired by the tried and true Nicholson bench. This design is robust and sturdy, built with hand tool work in mind. The legs are dadoed directly into the wide aprons, which makes it impossible for the bench to rack. The bench also doesn't use a vise to secure the work. There are many ways to hold on to components to work on them without using a vise. The shooting board/hook built in chapter 6 is is just one example.

Contrary to accepted convention, this bench is made of softwood. You can use wood from a home center or you can use pine from a wood seller. Either way, the bench is plenty heavy to stay put and stands up well against all of your woodworking processes. The softwood top is also a breeze to flatten, which you will need to do from time to time depending on the temperature and humidity swings where you live. Coming from a guy who has flattened a few hard maple benchtops, believe me when I say that this pine top is a joy to flatten.

TOOLS

pencil
ruler
square
panel saw
break-off-blade knife
divider
marking gauge
chisels
mallet
holdfast
brace and bit
screwdriver
bevel gauge
back saw
router plane
eggbeater drill
and ¾" bit
clamps
finishing rags

MATERIALS:

pine
PVA glue
#8 2" screws
¼" x 3" lag screws
and flat washers
#14 3" screws
boiled linseed oil or
polymerized tung oil

CUT LIST

PART	QUANTITY	THICKNESS	WIDTH	LENGTH	NOTES
Leg	4	3"	3½"	32½"	2 x 4s laminated
Upper stretcher	2	3"	3½"	19"	2 x 4s laminated
Lower stretcher	2	3"	3½"	18½"	2 x 4s laminated
Medial stretcher	1	1½"	3"	18"	—
Cleats	2	1½"	2"	6"	—
Apron	2	1½"	11½"	60"	—
Top	2	1½"	8¾"	60"	—

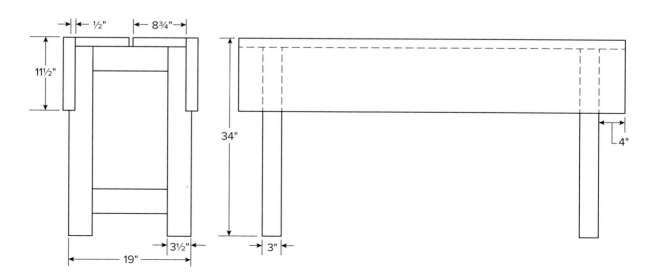

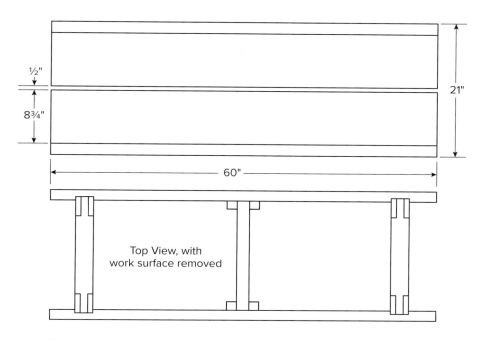

Top View, with
work surface removed

START WITH THE LEGS

1 Break out the material for the legs. Then glue and clamp up the two pieces for each leg. Once they dry, square-up the leg laminations and trim them to final length.

2 Decide on the orientation for the legs and mark the tops with a cabinetmaker's triangle.

MARK BRIDLE JOINTS AND MORTISES ON THE LEGS

3 To mark the joinery on the legs, you need the stretchers complete. Cut the pieces for the top and bottom stretchers and glue them together. Then bring them to final dimension and mark their orientation in sets of top and bottom stretchers using cabinetmaker's triangles.

4 Lay the top stretcher across the top of one set of legs, paying attention to your cabinetmaker's triangles. Using a knife, mark the width of the stretcher on the top of the legs. This mark establishes the depth of the bridle.

5 Divide the thickness of the leg into three, stepping it off with a divider.

PUT AWAY YOUR RULER

The top stretcher connects with the leg using a bridle joint and the lower stretcher connects to the lower part of the leg with a mortise and tenon joint. In both cases, use the dimensions of each actual component to mark the joinery. This technique of referential measurement eliminates the chance for errors in measuring.

6 Set a marking gauge to the width determined by the dividers and mark the cheeks of the bridle.

7 You can darken these lines with a pencil to make them easier to see.

8 Locate the mortise 4" from the bottom of the leg then lay the lower stretcher on this mark. Then, using the stretcher as your reference, mark the top of the mortise. Use the same marking gauge you used for the bridle to mark the mortises.

CUT THE MORTISE FOR THE BRIDLE JOINT

9

9 To cut the mortise for the bridle, use a panel saw cut on the waste side of the line to the base line.

10 Begin removing waste with a chisel by driving straight down ahead of the base line and coming in at 45° to remove a chunk of waste.

11 Keep doing this until you get halfway through, then flip the leg over and repeat the process until all the waste is gone. When the bulk of the waste is removed, place the chisel into the knife line and pare the last bit of waste away, ensuring that the chisel is straight as you go in.

10

11

WASTE OUT THE MORTISE
FOR THE HOUSED TENON

12 Mark out the mortise for the housed tenon using the same methods. Then hog out the bulk of the waste on the mortises using a brace and bit, leaving ¼" of material at the bottom.

13 Use your widest chisel to pare the remainder of the waste to the lines. Again, be sure to keep the chisel straight to ensure that the cheeks are square to the surface.

14 Monitor the squareness of the mortise with a small square and adjust as necessary.

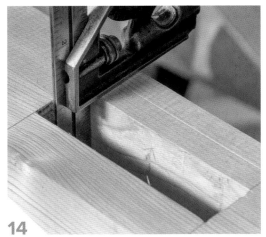

CUT THE TENONS

15

16

17

15 Lay the upper stretcher in line with the leg and transfer the mortise location onto the ends of the stretchers using a bevel gauge. This will ensure a tight fit because you are marking one piece directly off the other.

16 Set a marking gauge to these marks and carry the lines around the sides and the end. Be sure to do this step with each tenon in case there are slight differences. Then use the leg's width to mark the shoulder line of the tenon with a knife and mark your waste.

17 Make a saw groove on the shoulder line and saw to the line using a back saw.

18 Start removing the waste with a chisel and mallet. Pay attention to how the waste is coming off. If the waste is diving toward your lines, go slowly and take lighter cuts.

19 When you get close, switch to a cross-grain cut and bring the tenon cheek to the lines but no further. Sharp chisels are imperative at this point. It's difficult to remove wood with any precision if you're using a dull tool.

Test the fit often to ensure that you don't remove too much. Then repeat these steps for the lower tenon. Once all the joints are cut, dry assemble the parts to make sure everything goes together. Take it all apart again, because you will need the legs for the next steps.

PREPARE THE APRONS

20 Break out the aprons and cut them to final length. Then use a marking gauge to mark a line 4" from each end of each apron.

21 Lay the leg along the line and strike a knife line on the other side of the leg to set the width of the dado. Check the orientation of the leg to be sure you are marking off of the correct surface.

22 Set a marking gauge to the thickness of the bench top and use this measurement to mark the top of the dado.

23 Set a marking gauge to ½" and mark the depth of the dado. Repeat these steps for all the legs.

20

21

22

23

WASTE OUT THE DADO

24 Continue to deepen the cut until the depth line is reached.

25 Flip your widest chisel over so that the bevel is facing down and remove the bulk of the waste in the dado.

26 Set a router plane to the final depth and remove the last bit of waste. Be sure to check the shoulders of the dado for square and clean out any waste from the corners that could hold up the joint during assembly.

MAKE THE MEDIAL STRETCHERS

27 Create the blanks for the cleats that will support the medial stretchers. Then use the width of the medial stretcher to mark the width of the dado on the cleat. Mark halfway down the width of the cleat and connect all the layout lines.

28 Create saw grooves and saw down to the base line.

29 Saw a couple extra kerfs into the waste to make it easier to waste out.

30 Remove the waste with a chisel and mallet. Finish up with the chisel in the knife line for a final paring cut.

31 Mark a line vertically on the apron at the center. Mark a line horizontally from the top of the apron. This line depth is achieved by adding the width of the medial apron and the thickness of the stop. Glue and screw the cleat into place with two #8 screws.

27

28

29

30

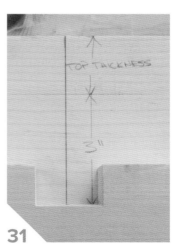

31

GLUE UP THE BASE

32 To glue up the leg assemblies, apply glue to the inside of the mortise.

33 Apply glue in the open mortises and then slide the tenons into place. Clamp the assemblies together until the glue dries.

34 Lay one apron on the floor and place the leg assemblies into the dados. Then clamp up the assemblies and let them dry.

35 After the assembly dries, place the other apron on the floor and flip the apron and legs over to install them into the second apron. This can be a bit tricky but if your joinery fits snugly you should be fine. Then take a seat on the apron and drill a ¾"-diameter counterbore, ½" deep.

GLUE UP THE BASE, *continued*

36 To avoid splitting the wood, drill the pilot hole for the lags to a depth of 3".

37 Drive the lags (with a flat washer) into the apron and legs with a ratchet.

38 Repeat this step for all four of the legs.

39 Trim the length of the medial stretcher to fit snuggly between the aprons and seat it all the way into the notch of the cleats. There is no need to glue or screw this in place because once the top is attached there is nowhere for it to go.

36

37

38

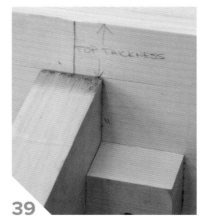

39

ATTACH THE TOP

40 Joint the edges of the two top pieces and lay them into place. Then mark the final length and trim the tops using a panel saw and a plane to clean them up. Once trimmed, clamp the first half of the top to the apron.

41 Drill pilot the holes for the #14 3" screws through the top of the bench and into the stretchers.

FINISH THE BENCH

Start flattening the top by first running the plane at a 45° angle to the apron from end to end, and then do the same in the opposite direction until all the surfaces have been cut by the plane. Then switch to end-to-end cuts to smooth the planing marks.

Finish for a workbench should be easy to reapply over the life of the bench. The finish for this bench couldn't be easier. Simply flood the surface with boiled linseed oil or polymerized tung oil and keep the surface wet for about 10 minutes. Then remove the excess oil with a clean rag. When working with oils, be sure not to ball up the used rags because they can auto-combust. The safest way to deal with them is to hang them up outside until they dry and then discard them when they are hard and crusty.

USING YOUR NEW BENCH

DOG HOLES
Many woodworkers tend to drill a matrix of holes in their workbench, making the top resemble Swiss cheese. I personally don't do this. I like drilling dog holes as I need them on the surface and apron. After working on your bench for a while, you will likely notice that you use the same set of holes repeatedly. I use a brace and ¾" bit to drill the holes, so the process is simple and only takes a minute to do.

WORKING ON THE FLAT
When working on the faces of boards, it isn't always necessary to pinch the board between a set of dogs. In fact, the only time I fully secure a board is when I am plowing a groove, rabbeting, or removing a large amount of stock, as is the case when flattening.

PLANING STOP
A planing stop is a simple bench accessory that gives you a surface to work up against. Light-duty tasks like smoothing are simple to do using a planing stop and you don't have to clamp and unclamp boards as you work.

Planing Stop

PLANING STOP & DOE'S FOOT
If you plan on exerting any lateral pressure on the board then add a doe's foot to the planing stop to ensure the board stays put. The way the doe's foot works almost seems magical and the simple addition of this bench accessory will eliminate the need for a tail vice. Making one couldn't be simpler. Cut a 90° notch at the end of a 1 x 3 piece of scrap and hold it down with a holdfast.

Planing Stop and Doe's Foot

HOLDFASTS

Holdfasts come in many shapes and styles and generally all work the same. The pad contacts the board you are trying to secure while the shaft wedges itself into a dog hole with the help of a sharp mallet blow. Some holdfasts have a mechanical tightening action which makes it easier to dial up the holding power you need.

Holdfasts

WORKING ON THE EDGE

Holding a board on edge is a common occurrence in woodworking especially when jointing a board. If the board's width is less than five times its thickness, you will be able to work against a stop alone.

If the board is wider than that, you can simply secure a woodscrew clamp to the benchtop with a holdfast and place the board into the clamp to secure it.

If you need more holding power then grab a couple of 12" "F" clamps and place the head in the split of your bench and tighten the other end on the board.

Planing Stop

Woodscrew Clamp and Holdfast

"F" Clamp

Chapter 9

HAND TOOL
SHELF

One of the most important things to consider when you work in a small space is effective storage of your tools. They should have a place to live that is out of the way yet be close enough to hand that you can grab them quickly. My most used tools sit on the shelf built in this chapter. Things like my jack plane, marking tools, and a few saws are the ones I use the most. I keep my other, less used tools in a mid-1800s chest that I inherited.

I chose oak for this particular build because it is strong and has a grain pattern that is pleasing to the eye. The shelf may be small in size but it will hold plenty of weight due to its solid joinery. The combination of dados that house the shelves and a saw hanger board that is notched into the gables gives this shelf an attractive look and a rock solid construction.

This design works well for most any tool set. Also, it can easily be modified in size for other uses elsewhere in the house. Whether you plan to use it to store your tools or to display your prized troll doll collection, this simple shelf will fit the bill.

TOOLS

pencil
ruler
square
panel saw
clamps
break-off-blade knife
marking gauge
chisels
mallet
router plane
back saw
compass
coping saw
block plane
smoothing plane
eggbeater drill and ⅛" bit
flush-cut saw

MATERIALS

red oak
painter's tape
paste wax
paper towels
PVA glue
⅛" hardwood dowels

CUT LIST

PART	QUANTITY	THICKNESS	WIDTH	LENGTH
Gable	2	⅝"	6"	26"
Shelves	3	⅝"	6"	17"
Saw Hanger	1	¾"	2"	17½"

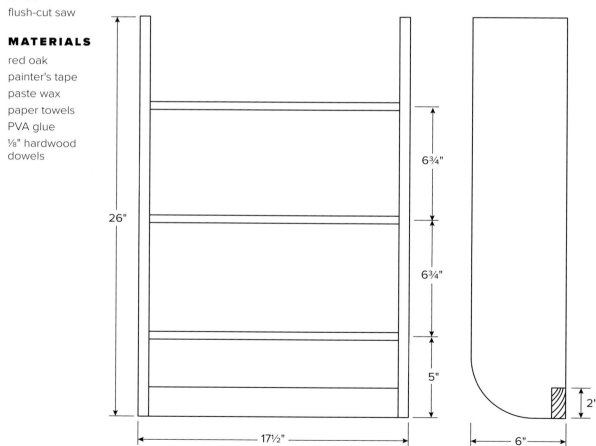

PREPARE AND MARK THE LUMBER

1

2

1 As with earlier projects in this book, the first step is to break out the lumber to the sizes in the cut list and mark your components with the cabinetmaker's triangle.

2 Clamp the two gable pieces together with the insides facing each other. Using a knife, scribe the locations of the shelves.

WORK OUT THE DADOS

3 Line up the shelf components with the centerlines you scribed and mark both sides of the shelf with a knife. Don't mark the whole width for now, just the edges. Place the knife into the marks that you have made and bring a square up to the knife. Scribe along the square, being sure to start with light passes and gradually deepen the knife line with subsequent cuts. Make sure that you have a good grip on your square so it doesn't move during the process.

4 Once you have marked all of the shelves on one gable, line up the two gables flat on your bench and transfer the shelf locations onto the second one. Use the same technique with the square and knife to bring those lines across. Then scribe the depth of the dado with the marking gauge.

5 Use a chisel to cut a saw groove with the angled edge on the inside of the dado. Just like the workbench (only on a much smaller scale), begin by removing the waste with a chisel, then follow up with the router plane to get a flat, consistent dado.

LET IN THE SAW HANGER BOARD

6

7

8

6 Using the saw hanger board, mark its location on the bottom back of the gables with a marking knife.

7 Set the marking gauge to the thickness of the saw hanger board— no need for measurements. Then scribe the thickness onto the gables. Be sure that the fence of the marking gauge stays engaged with the edge of the board. Sometimes gauges can wander on woods that have strong grain like oak.

8 Place your knife into the knife mark you made on the edge of the gable and bring a square up to the knife. Connect the edge knife line to the one you scribed with the marking gauge.

LET IN THE SAW HANGER BOARD, *continued*

9 Create a saw groove on the edge of the board then drop your back saw in the groove and saw down to the scribe line.

10 Rotate the board and saw down the grain to remove the rest of the waste. Be sure to use long strokes with the saw to help ensure a straight cut. You paid for the whole saw plate so you might as well use it.

11 Nobody is perfect. If your saw line was a bit off then pare the remaining waste with a chisel. Just be mindful of the scribe line and don't go past it.

9

10

11

WORK ON THOSE CURVES

12

12 Set the compass for a 4-inch radius and place the point in the position that lines the pencil up to the front edge and the bottom of the gable.. This setting should have the pencil hitting the edge and the end of the gable.

13 Use the coping saw to cut as close to the line as you dare to start shaping the curve. Like with any other saw, use the whole blade and don't force the cut. Not heeding this advice results in a wonky cut that needs more faring. Then grab your block plane and guide it along the curve to get rid of the saw marks and to fare the curve. Be sure to have the plane set for a light cut; most of the work is end-grain, so you'll want to take small bites.

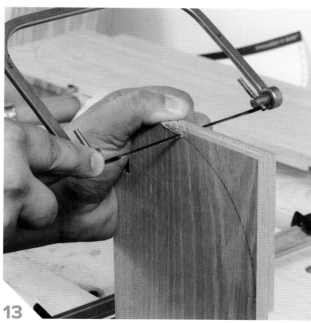

13

MAKE IT PRETTY

14 Set your smoothing plane for the lightest cut you can and do a final smoothing on all the parts. This step will remove any pencil marks, smudges, or dirt that have accumulated as you worked.

15 Because you are removing the pencil marks you have to mark the components somehow to ensure the assembly goes well. I like to use painter's tape with the cabinetmakers marks on them.

16 Apply a coat of paste wax with a paper towel, being sure to get an even coat on all the components. The paper towel will burnish the surface lightly, giving you a silky smooth surface with not a lot of shine. My favorite wax is a Canadian-made product called Clapham's Beeswax Polish. It's easy to apply and gives me a great result.

14

15

16

PUT IT ALL TOGETHER

17

18

17 Dry assemble the shelf and hold it all together with a clamp. Place the saw hanger in the notches and drill two ⅛" holes on each end for the dowels. We will be using a technique often used by Japanese woodworkers using wooden nails (dowels) to fasten things together. This is a very durable technique and the end-grain from the dowels looks great. Shoot for a depth of approximately 1½" to 2" for the pilot holes.

Drop some glue into the pilot holes and gently tap the wood nails into the holes

until they bottom out. You'll know this has happened because the sound of the hammer tap will deepen in pitch . . . that and the dowel won't go any further.

18 You can use any saw to trim the dowels but I prefer to use a flush-cut saw. A back saw can do the trick; you just need to be careful that you don't scratch up the surface with the set of the saw. If the dowels still protrude, then flush them up with a chisel laid flat on the surface using a paring cut.

PUT IT ALL TOGETHER, *continued*

19 For the shelves, place a piece of painter's tape across the width of the gable roughly centered on the shelf. Then use a square lined up with the center of the shelf and mark the center on the tape. This will allow you to line up the wooden nails while not marking up the freshly planed surfaces.

20 Install three wooden nails along the line in the same manner as the ones on the saw hanger. I used my thumb width to mark the distance from the edge for the outer two holes, then placed another mark centered between the two. Finally, use a chisel to pare the wooden nails flush with the surface.

19

20

HANGING AND FILLING

This shelf will hold a ton of weight so I opted for heavy-duty, screw-in drywall anchors and # 8 screws to attach it to the wall. Attach an L-bracket to the underside of the top shelf and mount it in place.

You can see what I chose to put on the shelves in the photo. These are the tools I use most and wanted them close by so I don't have to search for them. The saws hang on wine corks with screws through them. The cork makes sure that your saw handles don't get beat up and provides a cushy resting place. You can find unused corks at winemaking and craft supply stores, or you can do what I do and buy a few bottles of wine . . . for the corks of course.

The smaller Gent's saw and hook ruler are held in place with of magnetic studs I screwed into a pilot hole. I also mounted a small hooks to the outside to hold my corn broom and bench brush. The tools on your shelf are up to you.

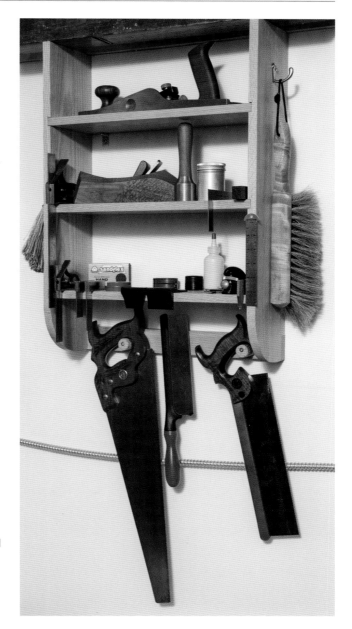

SUMMARY

So there you have it. You have the fixtures, tools, and furniture to outfit your corner of the woodworking world. I hope that I've convinced you that you don't need every tool under the sun just to woodwork. You also don't need vast amounts of space to woodwork. It's true that you won't be making king-sized beds or an 18-seater dining table . . . but you'll certainly be making.

Your next steps in your journey could be box making to provide a home for some of those special tools or perhaps some storage for nails, screws, and other hardware.

Making custom boxes is a great way to practice your newly acquired skills and they make effective storage for your work space. I love small wooden boxes for the odds and sods that can easily get out of control. Making your own wooden storage containers also prevents you from having to buy/use plastic ones. Before you know it you will be making well-built little boxes for your shop and can branch out to boxes for other uses around the house.

The most important thought I want to leave you with has to do with improving. There is only one way that I know of to effectively get better at woodworking—practice. The more time you spend with a saw in your hand, the straighter you will cut. Spend time sharpening your tools and amazingly they will be keen and ready to go at all times. Pay attention to setting your planes and you will soon be removing gossamer-thin shavings from your work. Forget about the notion of 'perfection' and start making things. Wooden objects made in production facilities lead us to believe that every surface must be pristine and free of minor flaws. This is not an easily achievable goal when working with hand tools alone. So embrace the 'character' in your work and keep on learning.

In order to understand, you must do. — VIC TESOLIN

IMPERIAL TO METRIC CONVERSION

Inches	mm*	Inches	mm*	Inches	mm*
1/32	0.79	17/32	13.49	2	50.8
3/64	1.19	35/64	13.89	3	76.2
1/16	1.59	9/16	14.29	4	101.6
5/64	1.98	37/64	14.68	5	127.0
3/32	2.38	19/32	15.08	6	152.4
7/64	2.78	39/64	15.48	7	177.8
1/8	3.18	5/8	15.88	8	203.2
9/64	3.57	41/64	16.27	9	228.6
5/32	3.97	21/32	16.67	10	254.0
11/64	4.37	43/64	17.07	11	279.4
3/16	4.76	11/16	17.46	12	304.8
13/64	5.16	45/64	17.86	13	330.2
7/32	5.56	23/32	18.26	14	355.6
15/64	5.95	47/64	18.65	15	381.0
1/4	6/35	3/4	19.05	16	406.4
17/64	6.75	49/64	19.45	17	431.8
9/32	7.14	25/32	19.84	18	457.2
19/64	7.54	51/64	20.24	19	482.6
5/16	7/94	13/16	20.64	20	508.0
21/64	8.33	53/64	21.03	21	533.4
11/32	8.73	27/32	21.43	22	558.8
23/64	9.13	55/64	21.83	23	584.2
3/8	9.53	7/8	22.23	24	609.6
25/64	9.92	57/64	22.64	25	635.0
13/32	10.32	29/32	23.02	26	660.4
27/64	10.72	59/64	23.42	27	685.8
7/16	11.11	15/16	23.81	28	711.2
29/64	11.51	61/64	24.21	29	736.6
31/64	11.91	31/32	24.61	30	762.0
1/2	12.70	63/64	25.00	31	787.4
33/64	13.10	1 inch	25.40	32	812.8

*Rounded to nearest 0.01 mm

ABOUT THE AUTHOR

Before he jumped into the world of woodworking, Vic Tesolin served 14 years in the Royal Canadian Horse Artillery. After leaving the RCHA on an honorable discharge, he studied furniture design/making at Rosewood Studio and learned from some of the best in the business, including Garrett Hack and Michael Fortune. After finishing up his studies, Vic owned his own studio while working part-time at Rosewood as an instructor and craftsman in residence before eventually becoming an editor at *Canadian Woodworking* magazine. Vic now has the very cool job of working as a Technical Adviser for a prominent woodworking retailer. He also builds what he wants, when he wants, in his minimalist workshop. Learn more about Vic and check out his blog, latest projects, and other cool stuff at the MinimalistWoodworker.com.

ACKNOWLEDGEMENTS

I have been fortunate to have studied under some of the finest craftsmen of this time and I am always thankful to have had those opportunities. Perhaps the most influential in my woodworking is Ron Barter at my alma mater, Rosewood Studio. Ron taught me many things (good and bad) but chiefly that anything is possible, no mistake is too big to fix, and single malt whiskey is always appropriate. Having a teacher like Ron makes me content being a lifelong student.

Index

NOTE: Page numbers in *italics* indicate projects.

MORE GREAT BOOKS *from* SPRING HOUSE PRESS

Classic Wooden Toys
ISBN: 978-1-940611-34-1
$24.95 | 200 Pages

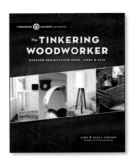

The Tinkering Woodworker
ISBN: 978-1-940611-08-2
$24.95 | 160 Pages

Getting Started in Woodturning
ISBN: 978-1-940611-09-9
$27.95 | 224 Pages

The Handmade Skateboard
ISBN: 978-1-940611-06-8
$24.95 | 160 Pages

The New Bandsaw Box Book
ISBN: 978-1-940611-32-7
$19.95 | 128 Pages

The Cocktail Chronicles
ISBN: 978-1-940611-17-4
$24.95 | 200 Pages

THE ILLUSTRATED WORKSHOP SERIES

Furniture Design & Construction
ISBN: 978-1-940611-05-1
$24.95 | 256 Pages

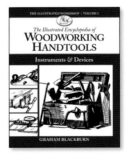

**Illustrated Encyclopedia of
Woodworking Handtools**
ISBN: 978-1-940611-02-0
$24.95 | 192 Pages

SPRING HOUSE PRESS

Look for these Spring House Press titles at your favorite bookstore or woodworking retailer.
For more information or to order direct, visit *www.springhousepress.com* or call 717-208-3739.